Globalisation
and the
New Realities

Globalisation
and the
New Realities

Selected Speeches of
DR MAHATHIR MOHAMAD
Prime Minister of Malaysia

Edited by
HASHIM MAKARUDDIN

Globalisation and the New Realities
Selected Speeches of Dr Mahathir Mohamad
Prime Minister of Malaysia

Published by
Pelanduk Publications (M) Sdn Bhd
(Co. No. 113307-W)
12 Jalan SS13/3E, Subang Jaya Industrial Estate
47500 Subang Jaya, Selangor Darul Ehsan, Malaysia

for the
Prime Minister's Office of Malaysia
Putrajaya, Malaysia

Visit us at *www.pelanduk.com*
e-mail: *mypp@tm.net.my*

Mahathir bin Mohamad, Dato' Seri, 1925-
    Globalisation and the new realities: selected speeches of Dr
    Mahathir Mohamad, Prime Minister of Malaysia / edited by
    Hashim Makaruddin.
    ISBN 967-978-818-0
    1. Globalisation. 2. International relations. 3. Speeches,
    addresses, etc. I. Hashim Makaruddin. II. Title.
    303.482

Printed and bound in Malaysia

Contents

5

Foreword

"The fact that globalisation has come does not mean we should just sit by and watch as the predators destroy us," Dr Mahathir reiterates. Policymakers, researchers and those who want to know about the current trends in globalisation—and about its perils—will find this timely and interesting reading.

THIS collection of recent speeches and writings on globalisation by Malaysia's Prime Minister, Dato Seri Dr Mahathir Mohamad, makes for compelling reading. There are several reasons for this. In the past few years there has been a worldwide public backlash against the effects of globalisation, which had once been thought of as an inevitable and universally good force. These speeches provide an incisive critique of the main aspects of globalisation and thus an explana-

7

tion for this changing tide of opinion against the dominant form of globalisation.

But this is not just another book on the pitfalls of globalisation. It is written by a political leader of a developing country who has been warning the world of the inequities and dangers of globalisation years before it was fashionable to criticise this concept and process. Dr Mahathir became a prominent spokesperson of the South on this subject.

It will be obvious to the reader that many of the ideas and conclusions in these speeches are drawn from Dr Mahathir's personal experiences and knowledge as a leader whose country has recently gone through the trauma of an unexpected financial and economic crisis caused primarily by the forces of financial globalisation. Thus the many insights found here could not have come from only an intellectual study of the subject. In many speeches, one gets a good sense of his intense grappling with the difficult policy aspects and events relating to Malaysia's response to the developments and pressures of globalisation.

The policy choices taken by a developing country in responding to the challenge of globalisation (and in its relations with the world market) have an enormous impact on its economic, social and political life. Dr Mahathir's thinking on globalisation has attracted international attention not only because he is one of the few political leaders in the world who has criticised current globalisation trends in his characteristic frank and blunt manner, but even more so because of the bold and unorthodox policies taken by Malaysia at the height of the financial and economic crisis of 1997-99 to counter financial speculation and to revive the economy that had been on the verge of collapse.

Malaysia was the only country facing the crisis at that time to reject IMF-type policies and to devise its own package of policies that included a fixed exchange rate, deinternationalising the currency, selective exchange and capital controls, including a temporary moratorium on outflow of foreign portfolio capital, reduction of interest rates and expansion of public spending. As Malaysia did not resort to the IMF, it was also able to avoid being forced to have an open-door policy for the foreign purchase of local assets as happened in other countries. Since the homegrown policies did contribute to a recovery, many people around the world have been interested to find out about the Malaysian alternative to the orthodox IMF structural adjustment policies, which pressurise its client countries to adopt a "one-size-fits-all" opening up to the world market.

Since Dr Mahathir is the prime architect of the Malaysian "alternative approach" to economic recovery, his thinking and writings on globalisation take on added significance. He makes clear in this book that his attack on the system is that of a believer. He believes in the market system, capitalism and globalisation, and gives data showing that Malaysia is amongst the half-dozen most globalised and open countries in the world. His criticism is that the major players in the system have devised unfair rules of the game for their own benefit, keeping developing countries out of the benefits and causing them to lose out.

Dr Mahathir's criticism is that "globalisation" is a concept devised by and made use of by powerful countries to open up the economies of weaker countries. The products, big companies and banks of the developed countries can then enter the developing countries and take control of them as local products and small local firms fall under the onslaught of trade and investment liberalisation. He strongly criticises the IMF for acting on behalf of the rich countries, for its disastrous policies and its meddling in local affairs. He also points out the wrong approach taken by the WTO in treating all countries as if they have the same capacity, and warns that the developed countries are lining up "Trojan Horses" of new agreements that will cause developing countries to lose their capacity to make their own national socioeconomic policies. "Globalisation can therefore result in loss of economic, political and social independence," he warns.

Dr Mahathir admits that foreign trade and direct investment has greatly benefited Malaysia, but he is worried that protectionist policies in the rich countries and the pressures they exert to get developing countries to liberalise further is leading to unequal benefits and potential losses. And he comes out strongly against the free flow of short-term capital, the free convertibility of currencies and the free market in currencies as the most damaging features of globalisation.

He is most eloquent when he describes the events of the Asian crisis, the mechanics of currency speculation and the effects of the volatile inflows and outflows of foreign funds, as well as the measures Malaysia took to counter the crisis.

In this book, the reader will also find an outline of Dr Mahathir's antidote to uncontrolled or unfettered globalisation. The present globalisation must be questioned and should not be left to the rich countries to determine. And developing countries must act together to demand a say in making decisions that shape globalisation. Globalisation must be governed by rules and practices that protect poor countries from repeated economic turmoil. Handicaps must be given to the disadvantaged. Governments must regulate. Currency trade must be made transparent and a limit be put on it to prevent excesses. And a tax should be imposed on all international speculators.

"The fact that globalisation has come does not mean we should just sit by and watch as the predators destroy us," Dr Mahathir reiterates. Policymakers, researchers and those who want to know about the current trends in globalisation—and about its perils—will find this timely and interesting reading.

Martin Khor
Director
Third World Network

1

Globalisation: Challenges and Impact on Asia

"The challenge for Asia is not how to manage the present concept of globalisation but to make it work and to benefit from it. The challenge for Asia is to influence the thinking on globalisation, to reshape it, to reduce the chances of it going awry and destroying economies and countries."

"GLOBALISATION" is a word that seems to describe the coming together of all the countries of the globe into one entity. It was coined by the rich countries, apparently in response to technological advances and the speed and ease of travel. But the emphasis appears to be on the free flow of capital and

A speech delivered at the World Economic Forum (WEF) in New York on February 3, 2002 trade in goods and services. People and other things may not flow so freely.

Free means free of governmental regulations, laws and policies. International institutions would take over, enact rules and enforce them. Looked at from the viewpoint of weak countries, rules, laws and policies will still exist but they will have no say in their determination or enforcement.

But for most of the developing countries, globalisation means not more freedom but less freedom from rules, regulations, laws and policies. Worse still, these uniform rules, regulations, laws and policies disregard their particular weaknesses and problems.

But they are being told that being poor, they will benefit from capital flowing into their countries. In fact, for many of the East Asian countries, capital inflows have brought about unprecedented economic growth. Even their stock markets have benefited from foreign investments. But what they are not told is that the same capital can flow out and when it does their countries can be bankrupted.

It is unfortunate that East Asian countries learnt about this through experience and they now know how terrible the damage is and how difficult it is to recover.

The East Asian financial crisis was precipitated by the free exit of capital which started with the manipulative devaluation of the currencies of these countries. Devaluation caused foreign investments to lose value. To avoid losses from further devaluation, foreign capital was pulled out. The market collapsed, resulting in a rapid increase of non-performing loans, deprivation from bank funding of business operations, numerous bankruptcies and failure of the banking system in the end.

With the economy in tatters, the government had to borrow from the International Monetary Fund (IMF), but loans would only be given if the government surrenders economic management to the IMF and allows foreign white knights to pick up the devalued local banks and businesses.

Many countries are floundering because the money they borrowed from the IMF had to be used to pay off foreign creditors. Nothing is left for the locals. Of course, they still have to pay the IMF for the loans they had borrowed.

While East Asian countries are recovering from its slump (where some have made a fair degree of recovery), countries like Argentina are not so lucky. Sovereign loans are not so safe after all as countries can go bankrupt when the IMF imposes its policies.

Clearly, what happened to the East Asian countries is a manifestation of globalisation. Trading in currencies is only possible if government abdicates as the authority to determine the value of currency and leaves it to so-called international market forces. The market is interested only in making profits and cares nothing for the wellbeing of society.

The market favours the rich and the technologically advanced. Today, banks and corporations are merging and acquiring each other to become even bigger. Quite naturally the bigger banks and corporations are not going to be from developing countries.

When all the borders are down, these super giants will move in to gobble up all local businesses and will ignore the interests of the countries where they operate. Their only concern is to make money. If they have to pull out of a country in order to reduce losses and maximise profits, they will do so without compunction. It is irrelevant to them if their pulling out precipitates economic turmoil, massive unemployment and bankruptcies. It is regarded as the fault of these countries.

Being big is all-important: it guarantees success, ensures economies of scale, more research and development, and cheaper products. But we have seen that size did not save Long-Term Capital Management (LTCM) or Enron. Indeed, the bigger they are, the harder they fall, dragging everyone down with them.

The kind of globalisation promoted by the rich western countries has not convinced Asia that this is the answer to economic ills or the vitamin for economic growth.

Globalisation need not be about free capital flows only. Regulated globalisation—one that is not absolutely free nor purely market driven—can still be compatible with today's idea or concept of globalisation.

The challenge for Asia is not how to manage the present concept of globalisation but to make it work and to benefit from it. The challenge for Asia is to influence the thinking on globalisation, to reshape it, to reduce the chances of it going awry and in the process destroying economies and countries.

There is nothing sacred about the present concept of globalisation that it cannot be changed, radically if necessary, so that it poses less danger to those accepting and practising it. Free trade is not synonymous with globalisation. If we have to regulate trade in order to benefit from globalisation, why not?

People who play golf know that there will never come a time when handicaps will be abolished. In business, too, fair competition can only be between entities of fairly equal strength because level playing fields are not enough. The contestants must be evenly matched. If we cannot match them, then give them handicaps.

Prior to 1997, the Asian countries were growing miraculously. Malaysia registered a growth rate of 8 per cent plus per annum for ten consecutive years. Today, every one of these miracle economies are shadows of their former selves. The impact of globalisation involving the free flow of capital and the straightjacketing of business has been disastrous.

For years now attempts to resuscitate the economies have not been very successful. There will be permanent scars and the impact will not be any better for as long as the present interpretation of globalisation is forced upon Asia. In fact, the world is likely to fail to recover if, instead of focusing on resuscitating the economy following the September 11 bombing of the World Trade Center in New York and the Pentagon in Washington, D.C., it continued to impose its version of globalisation on the rest of the world.

17

2

Islam and Globalisation

"Muslims and Muslim countries are faced with a tremendous and frightening challenge. Globalisation in the form that it takes now is a threat against us and our religion. We should not vent our anger and frustration by mounting futile isolated violence. Instead, we should plan and execute the development of our *ummah* so as to be empowered by information technology and be capable of handling the challenges of the Information Age."

GLOBALISATION, as it is formulated and presented today, is an invention of the North Atlantic countries, and we can take it for granted that it is intended to enrich them further and enhance their domination of the world. They already dominate the world, of course. But they want to strengthen that domi-

---

A speech delivered at the meeting with Muslim intellectuals and businessmen in Doha, Qatar, on November 11, 2001

nation to ensure they will not be successfully challenged either by the big East Asian countries or even the weak Muslim countries.

The peoples of Europe have always been an aggressive and acquisitive people. Before they were able to cross the oceans, they were continuously fighting each other and trying to occupy each other's land in Europe. In the past two millenniums not a year passed when they were not fighting each other.

Their whole culture and economy was based on wars of conquest. They were always thinking of and inventing more and better weapons to kill people. Even today we see them inventing newer infernal machines for killing people more efficiently. Whenever they can they would test these weapons in other countries, causing death by the tens or even hundreds of thousands. Their excuse now is that they want to keep the world safe for peace.

After they learned how to navigate the oceans they turned their aggressive acquisitiveness against the rest of the world. By the beginning of the last century almost every part of the world had come under their rule. Practically every European nation had some territory to call their colony. Asia, Africa and the Americas were not only subjected to their imperious and frequently brutal rule but had all their wealth and resources taken away to enrich the metropolitan countries. Europeans treated other races of the world as inferior and in many cases simply exterminated them. In Australia the aborigines were shot on sight like animals. The Tasman Man is now extinct because of this. Of course, when they are doing this they did not talk about human rights. It would not serve their purpose.

After the end of World War II they began to give up their colonial territories. It was not because they had suddenly changed as they tried to make the world believe. It was simply because they feared defection by their colonial subjects to the other bloc as a result of their Cold War confrontation between the Western capitalists and the Eastern socialists.

Even as they were freeing their colonies they were consolidating themselves in order to ensure their continued dominance over the world. They closed ranks and formed the European Economic Community (EEC) which eventually became the European Union (EU). They also set up the North Atlantic Treaty Organisation (NATO) countries and finally when the Cold War ended in the defeat of the Eastern Bloc they coalesced and have now become a solid European entity led by the seven strongest countries amongst them.

Now they bared their capitalists fangs. No longer worried about the socialists, they propounded the religion of free trade. Free trade is everything. It is going to enrich the whole world. It is going to lead to a worldly paradise. Many have forgotten that they had also promised worldly paradise when they preached communism and absolute equality. Now they are back with the same promise and it looks like people are taken in by this old promise.

Free trade as enunciated by them means the removal of all trade barriers so that goods and services can move freely across borders. Free trade is described as levelling the playing field. The implication is that a level playing field would ensure fair competition. Nothing is said about the size of the players.

Such is their hype that many poor countries talked about level playing fields, forgetting that the poor own no giant corporations or banks or products to sell in the market. Clearly, only those who have money and products will corner the markets.

Insidiously free trade became sacrosanct through the General Agreement on Tariffs and Trade (GATT) and the World Trade Organisation (WTO). The World Bank, the IMF and the Western-controlled international media preached it. Anyone who dared to oppose free trade became heretics, infidels, non-believers who were trying to impoverish the poor.

The true meaning and implications of free trade did not become known until the free trade in currencies reached its peak during the East Asian financial crisis. Suddenly, rich emerging economies crumbled as their currencies were traded and devalued. The currency traders claimed that the economic system of these East Asian tigers were rotten, they were corrupt and practised cronyism. Because of that their currencies were unhappy and devalued themselves.

The fact, of course, is that the currency traders saw an opportunity to make huge profits by devaluing the currencies of these countries. They made billions of dollars simply by destroying the wealth which these countries had taken decades to build up. But more than that they impoverished millions of people, threw them on the streets, and caused them to riot, kill and overthrow their governments. To this day these once-rich people are wallowing in poverty and instability.

Despite clear evidence that free trade has caused unprecedented misery it is still being touted as the solution to the economic problems of the poor. Worse still, it has been upgraded and given a new name: *Globalisation, a world without borders*. And again we are being told that globalisation will enrich us all.

Let us examine a little the contents of globalisation. They include doing away with borders, i.e. countries will lose their definitive territories, will become just a name for a certain area of the globe. Countries can therefore no longer barricade themselves behind their borders to stop the invading hordes from the rich countries from trampling all over their puny corporations, banks and industries.

Ahead of the invasion their propaganda machines are already saying that the monopoly of all economic activities by these foreign giants would improve efficiency, the quality of the products and services that we get, and the quality of our life.

Maybe the quality of our life will improve; maybe we will earn more pay. But we will all be servants of foreigners. What is worse is that these huge foreign-owned businesses will control our economy and eventually our governments. We will become like the banana republics where the managers of foreign corporations are more powerful than our presidents or prime ministers. Indeed they will determine who our presidents and prime ministers will be.

At that stage can we honestly say we are still independent? Only the soft-brained amongst us will maintain that we are free countries in charge of our destinies. We have *de facto* become the colonies of the European nations again. We have come full circle.

At the beginning it was pointed out that when the Europeans came up with an idea, it is invariably intended to result in their domination over the world. Well, globalisation is their idea, and we can see how it is going to lead to their rebuilding their World Empire. The developing countries of the world will pay a high cost if they swallow European ideas unthinkingly.

All Muslim countries are developing countries and they will all become a part of the empire of the North Atlantic countries if globalisation as presently conceived goes through. The picture is grim but it is not an exaggeration. The Muslim countries are weak. None of them

23

have any influence over world affairs. For a century now they have suffered in silence while Muslims and Muslim countries are oppressed.

The situation in Palestine is typical. Children who threw stones are being shot dead with live bullets. Many have been killed. There is nothing that one billion Muslims in the world can do. We can send appeals to stop the carnage but all that we get is to be told to stop the children from throwing stones. No one tells the Israelis to stop shooting. It is as if the most natural thing for people to do when stones are thrown at them is to shoot the stone throwers dead. And yet these people who tolerate the killing of stone-throwing children talk endlessly about human rights, justice and the rule of law.

I have painted the gloomiest picture of globalisation, how it can oppress us, how it can make us once again the colonies of the rich. But it is not necessary that globalisation will have this kind of result. Globalisation can be made to work for us.

The first thing that we have do is to understand how globalisation as presently interpreted will work.

When Malaysia was being attacked by the currency traders we were shocked to find how little we knew about the international financial system; how currencies were traded; how money was moved without ever moving it physically.

Now we read about the hundreds of billions of dollars paid for companies by other companies wishing to grow by acquisition. We read about the mergers of the giants to become even bigger giants. We don't really know how they are doing this and where the money is coming from. They have found ways, or invented ways, to put huge sums of money to work for them.

If we know enough about these wheelings and dealings we may be able to play the same games, by our own rules. We may even be able to enter as a virus into their systems to paralyse or frustrate them. They are big but size alone will not guarantee that failures will not occur. They can fail. They can lose trillions of dollars. And they can destroy themselves in the process.

We know the story of the Long-Term Capital Management (LTCM), a huge hedge fund. It was huge. It dealt in billions. But suddenly it failed and but for the help of cronies in their government, it could have dragged the whole financial system of the rich down with it. If the giant banks and the giant corporations are skilfully handled, they too can suffer the same fate as the LTCM. And as they come crashing down they will drag the powerful countries down with them.

There was a time when Muslim countries dominated the world. Then there was a decline. The decline was because we were preoccupied with bickering amongst ourselves regarding the interpretations of our religion. Muslim governments are forever being attacked by extremist Muslims. Busy trying to defend their Islamic credentials, Muslims and their countries missed completely the Industrial Revolution which was taking place in the European world. We took no part in it and as a result we retrogressed, unable to gain anything from it. We became poor not just in terms of wealth but also in industrial capacities, the invention, design and production of the instruments of progress. We have become totally dependent on others even for our most simple needs, and the needs for our defence.

Now we are seeing the Information Age dawning upon the world. And it looks like we are going to miss this revolution, too. We are still too busy with our endless squabbles over our religion and our politics.

It is sad because we do have the capacity to participate in the development of information technology and its innumerable applications. Large numbers of highly skilled Muslims are now living in the countries of the North Atlantic. They are there because we have no place for them. And so they are contributing to the body of knowledge and Information Age skills being built up in these countries which may probably be used against us.

We can bring them back. We can tap their skills in order to build up our capacities in information technology. And with their skills and knowledge we may be able to counter some of the harmful effects of globalisation on us.

There are other ways we can work together to protect our economies and our countries. We can keep parts of our borders closed. We can stall everything until we are ready. We can change the interpretation of globalisation. We can, for example, interpret globalisation more completely by insisting on the rights of our poor people to cross into the rich countries.

That way we can reduce our poverty through the remittances of those of us who have gone abroad. It is important that Muslim communities abroad is big enough to maintain their religion and culture and possibly their influence in the countries of their adoption.

In a few decades the world's demography will change. There will be no country whose people are ethnically pure. If we are smart enough we can use this to our advantage.

Globalisation may result in huge corporations taking over the countries in which they operate. But, on the other hand, the migrants from the poor countries will, if not take over, at least play some role in the governance of the countries of their adoption. They may even be able to reduce the oppression of Muslims world-wide. Will Muslims lose in a global nation free of nation-states, including Muslim countries? They will lose if they insist on remaining as spectators. We are a billion strong. Every sixth person in this world is a Muslim. The real problem that we face in a globalised world is that we reject the brotherhood of Islam. Sadly, while others are uniting and consolidating their strength, we are fragmenting and drifting further and further apart.

Muslims and Muslim countries are faced with a tremendous and frightening challenge. Globalisation in the form that it takes now is a threat against us and our religion. We should not vent our anger and frustration by mounting futile isolated violence. Instead, we should plan and execute the development of our *ummah* so as to be empowered by information technology and be capable of handling the challenges of the Information Age. This is our real *jihad*. I believe we have the talents and the capacity to ensure the success of this *jihad*.

Allah does not help those who do not help themselves. Tie the camel and then leave it to Him. We have indeed to help ourselves, to tie our camels. We can quote the Quran and the Hadis and argue about their meaning but whatever the arguments may be we have to act to blunt the challenge of the globalised world. We may even master it and bring back the Golden Age of Islam.

3

Globalisation
With Common
Development

"... there is now a new global consensus that if
globalisation is to be sustainable, there must be many
more winners and many fewer losers, and they should
both be a mixture of the rich and the poor. There is a
new emerging global consensus that the winners must
not win to an obscene extent and the losers must not
lose to an equally obscene extent."

THERE is no doubt that one of the
great men of the 20th century was Deng Xiaoping, the
father of China's Four Modernisations. There is also no
doubt that two of his wise sayings should be in the forefront of our mind when we talk about the great public issues of our time, indeed when we talk of the great issues

A speech delivered at the APEC CEO Summit 2001 in Shanghai,
China, on October 20, 2001

of any time. They are an indispensable aid to analysis and an invaluable guide to action. They are very useful whether you are running a trade union, a multinational corporation or a country.

Deng said that we should seek truth from facts. That means that we should not deduce truth from our hopes, however noble. We should not deduce truth from our expectations, however certain. Or from conventional wisdoms of the day, however widely held. Or from the edicts of theologians, however exalted. Or from the simple ideology of the ideologues, however persuasive. We should deduce truth from facts.

Deng also said that it does not matter whether the cat is black or white so long as it catches mice.

In simple words, we must be pragmatic. This does not mean that the end justifies the means. But it does mean that we must be focused on results, on the true objectives that our societies must achieve. We must not be overly enchanted and loyal to the means that we have devised so much so that we forget the objectives. There is little virtue in pursuing the seemingly virtuous means if the results are perverse. We must be very fast on our feet, able to quickly adjust to changing circumstances. No single shoe can fit every foot. We must do what works for us. And when something no longer works for us, we must go to other strategies, policies and measures—quickly.

I stress the importance of the principle of deducing truth from facts because when it comes to the subject of "globalisation" today, the world faces a massive "truth deficit". There are too few facts and too much self-serving fiction. There are too many who are prepared to tell lies and to bend the truth to push through their sacred cause.

I stress the need for pragmatism because when we come to globalisation today, there is much too much ideology. There is too little common sense and straight thinking. The "pragmatism shortfall" is as profound as the "truth deficit". Whether we are Americans or Armenians, Swedes or Somalis, in or out of government, we all need less "group-think" and more independent thinking. And we must make sure that we are not being led by the nose, by well-meaning and not so well-meaning missionaries, some of whom have obviously gone through some of the world's best bible schools.

This is why I must congratulate the organisers for choosing the subject of my speech: "Globalisation with Common Development".

Apparently, the organisers do not think that globalisation (as it is being promoted, practised and pressed today) is working hard enough for our common good, for our common development. Not so long ago, this attitude would have constituted an impertinence, on the part of unrepentant, stubborn, ignorant recalcitrants who simply will not see the sacred truths.

The ideologies of globalisation have proselytised that globalisation is good for everyone, at all times, in every way. This is contrary to the facts, as experienced by many countries in East Asia, Africa and Latin America.

At the World Economic Forum in Davos, Switzerland, in February 1999, in the very heart of the heartland of today's globalisation ideology, Nelson Mandela asked the question: "Is globalisation only to benefit the powerful and the financiers, speculators, investors and traders? Does it offer nothing to men and women and children ravaged by the violence of poverty?"

Let me quote Mike Moore, Director-General of the World Trade Organisation. In November 2000, *The*

Economist, a committed ideologue on globalisation, quoted Moore as saying: "Sometimes I feel like joining the kids outside. When they say the system's unfair, they're not always wrong."

Not too long ago, the proponents of capitalism and the free market, including the WTO, exhorted: *"There can only be winners. Just endure the pain a little longer."* And a little longer and a little longer, and the gain must surely come. But it is now clear beyond any doubt that in the process of globalisation, as it is now promoted, practised and pressed on us, there are big winners and big losers and the basic pattern of winners and losers is unchanging—and unfair; for the winners are invariably the rich countries and the losers the poor ones.

Amongst the sensible and responsible thinkers who have a broad as opposed to a narrow perspective, there is now a new global consensus that if globalisation is to be sustainable, there must be many more winners and many fewer losers, and they should both be a mixture of the rich and the poor. There is a new emerging global consensus that the winners must not win to an obscene extent and the losers must not lose to an equally obscene extent.

The topic of my speech, given to me by the somewhat agnostic organisers, suggests that we must promote, practise and press an enlightened form of globalisation that is caring and productive for all, an enlightened globalisation that will ensure the common development of all; the common development of all not only across the world but also within our individual countries.

If we leave too many of the disempowered and the disadvantaged behind, globalisation cannot hold. Nor can it even be defended. Instead, it will become, as it already has in many circles, a swear word. Like so many other great ideas, it too will end up in the dustbin of history.

So far, there is no doubt who are the biggest winners in the game of globalisation: the very rich and the very empowered (and therefore the very immediately competitive). There is also absolutely no doubt about who are the biggest losers: the very poor and the very disempowered (those who haven't a ghost of a chance of competing right now with the best, the brightest, the most powerful, and the most endowed in the world).

The very rich today are called "HNWIs"—high net worth individuals.

Merrill Lynch and CAP Gemini Ernst & Young have issued, for several years now, a study they call the World Wealth Report. This year's World Wealth Report 2001, released in June, states that there were 7.2 million high net worth individuals last year, high net worth individuals being defined as people with investable assets of at least US$1 million, not counting real estate. These are people who have US$1 million or more that they can quickly put into stocks and shares, hedge funds, currency speculation, bonds and other financial instruments. It does not refer to the many more people who are less rich, who have incomes or assets above US$1 million.

Let me make it perfectly clear. I have nothing against rich people, against very rich people or against people who used to be called "the filthy rich". I hope that there are many in this audience who fall into one of these categories. I hope that those of us who are now not rich will one day be rich. I hope that those who are only rich today will be even richer in the days ahead. Deng was right in stressing the virtue of legitimately making a profit. Making money—without making misery—is indeed virtuous.

But you might be interested to know that since 1986, the combined wealth of the world's high net worth individuals have shot up three-fold, by more than 375 per cent.

In a "good" year like 1999, the total investable funds of the high net worth individuals identified by Merrill Lynch and CAP Gemini Ernst & Young grew by 18 per cent. Their investable wealth grew by US$4,000 billion. In other words, their additional wealth rose by four times the total GDP of China in 1999. In other words, the investable funds of these 7 million high net worth individuals grew by four times the good and service produced by 1.2 billion Chinese in China in 1999.

In a relatively "bad" 2000, when equity markets worldwide were subjected to high volatility, the world's high net worth individuals increased their additional investable wealth by only US$1,580 billion, an increase of only 6 per cent over the previous year. This might seem to be somewhat modest. Almost a paltry amount, in comparative terms, one might say, except that US$1,580 billion is almost three and a half times the total 2000 GDP of India, which has more than 1,000 million people.

After the events of September 11, I do not know whether global capital will be able to flow so freely across the globe, without national constraints or boundary obstacles. But on the assumption of present levels of globalisation of world financial markets, the World Wealth Report 2001 forecasts that over the next five years, the world's high net worth individuals will achieve an annual 8 per cent growth in their investable wealth. The extra wealth they are forecast to accumulate will bring the amount that they can put into stock markets, hedge funds, currency speculation, bonds and other financial instruments to US$39 trillion in 2005.

God only knows how much their total assets are worth. God only knows how much they can borrow. But last year, the 7 million rich people in the world had in their hands capital to invest amounting to 2.7 times the total goods and services produced by the almost 280 million citizens of the United States. If the World Wealth Report 2001 is correct in its predictions, by 2005 the amount that the world's high net worth individuals have for quickly investing in stocks, in the world's 6,000 hedge funds (which can in addition borrow massive amounts), in currency speculation, in bonds and other financial activities will be equivalent to 4 times the present GDP of the United States, 36 times the present GDP of China and 82 times the present GDP of India.

Imagine the enormous economic influence of these high net worth individuals on national governments and on the international financial system. They are the biggest beneficiaries of globalisation, with the biggest vested interests in the freest flow and the fullest free play of global capital. If I had a billion US dollars, I suspect I too would be very committed to a fully globalised world without any barriers and without any constraints on what I can do with my money and how I can make even more money.

Add to this the second biggest beneficiaries of globalisation as it is promoted, practised and pressed today: the global corporations who maximally seek global dominance, who minimally seek the greatest profitability and the maximisation of what they call "shareholder value".

I will say little about the multinational corporations, which we are all struggling to attract to our economies. It is sufficient to note that of the largest 100 economic entities in the world, 51 are global corporations and 49 are countries. The combined sales of the world's top 200 corporations exceed the combined GDPs of 182 of the world's nation-states. (Incidentally, they employ a total of only 18.8 million people, less than three-fourths of one per cent of the world's workers).

Given the mountain of money and the power that comes out of the almighty dollar, is it any surprise that global capitalism is in charge of the "Washington consensus", of the IMF, of the World Bank, of the WTO, of the wealthiest and most powerful nations of the world? Is it any surprise that global capitalism is in charge of the evolution of globalisation as it is today promoted, practised, and promoted? And can it be any surprise that what we have seen are forms of globalisation that work very hard for the very rich, that don't work very hard for the interests of the poor and the very poor, that work without any commitment or enthusiasm for the common development of the global community of mankind?

All thinkers of sense and sensibility must know that the present situation cannot stand. The world simply will no longer stand for it. But how do we get better results for all? I am afraid I see little hope for an effective global coalition that can work effectively for a more productive, compassionate and caring globalisation. There is very little hope for a global concert working for the enlightened globalisation that will, if I can paraphrase Nelson Mandela, offer much "to men and women and children ravaged by the violence of poverty."

We live in a world where the power of persuasion has too small a punch and where the persuasion of power packs too big a wallop. The rich and the powerful are in full command. They will concede what they must to get what they want. But they will yield little ground. Too many believe that utter selfishness is a virtue, that greed is great, that enlightened caring and compassion is a weakness, that selflessness and sacrifice for the common good is a mental illness.

Obviously, we have a much better chance of evolving a more productive globalisation if Asia unites behind the idea of productive, caring and compassionate globalisation. We must work hard to establish an Asian monetary system. We must work towards a stable Asian currency. We must cast off the traditional mind frame of "beggar thy neighbour" and replace it with the ethic of "prosper thy neighbour".

If our friends elsewhere are not willing to help, they should not seek to hinder. If they cannot be part of the solution, they should get out of the way and not be part of the problem.

Let me end by stressing a most obvious reality: the progress that we need in the years ahead can only come from national action and individual initiative.

We did not fight to be free in order to learn to "kowtow." We have a right to work for the benefit of our people and our future.

We must welcome advice, but we must not tolerate dictation. We must seek truth from facts. We must do what works and abandon what no longer does. It is true if you open the window to let in fresh air, some flies will enter. We should leave the windows open. But if we open the window and packs of tigers and bears enter, perhaps we should open the windows on the second floor and keep those on the ground floor securely closed. We should do this even in the face of the most seductive assurances of the bears and tigers. We should do this even in the face of the strongest opposition from the bears and tigers.

We must be prepared to quickly say yes to certain forms of globalisation. And we must be prepared to say no, no and no when we must, guided always by the dictates of pragmatism.

We in East Asia have benefited a great deal from some aspects of globalisation and also suffered a great deal from other aspects (as it is promoted, practised and pressed upon us today). We must work hard to improve the equation of costs and benefits.

As societies, we know that education and knowledge are essential for competitiveness in a globalising world. We must make sure that we make the necessary investment in the most important resource of our nations: our people.

And in the final analysis, we must make sure our people understand that the helping hand that every human being needs is the one at the end of his own right arm. After all, God only helps those who help themselves.

This was so before the age of globalisation. It is so today. It will always be so in the days ahead.

Above all, as Deng advised, we must seek truth from facts. We must do what works and abandon what no longer does. We must have the strength and the courage to do what is productive and good for our people and for the global community of mankind. Globalisation's promise of universal prosperity is illusory—a pragmatic approach to its proponents' demands is wisest.

4

Globalisation and its Impact on Developing Economies

"It is blatantly clear that if globalisation is to proceed apace—without a war in the streets—we need a new globalisation that works less diligently in the service of the very wealthy and much harder in the service of the very poor—between nations and within nations."

I have been asked to speak on globalisation and its impact on developing economies, focusing specifically on the key challenges that confront the developing world and the key responses that must be made.

A speech delivered at the 10th World Economic Development Congress in Kuala Lumpur, Malaysia, on June 27, 2001

Let me apologise for not being hypocritical and for
not saying some of the things that some may wish me to
say. I am tempted to try but as a medical doctor I am a
little worried about the effects of a physiological process
called "choking". I am sure you would not want me to
choke on my words and to collapse right before your
very eyes.

Let me also apologise for saying some politically incorrect things. We so obviously live in a world where
some things are politically correct and where some
things are politically incorrect. The sacred truths of the
new economic religion called "globalisation" or the
"market system" or "neo-liberalism" are very simple
and completely clear. The penalty for any developing-
country leader who does not get up every morning to de-
claim these sacred truths, and the punishment for any
developing-country leader who does not go to bed each
night without declaiming these sacred truths, are altogether well known. I will not tell you the intimate details
of what I do when I get up in the morning and what I do
before retiring at night. But I must apologise to those
who are offended by the fact that I am not a wide-eyed
believer in this new religion—a religion which so insis-
tently demands complete, unquestioning belief and
complete, unquestioning obedience—especially from
the poor and the weak, especially when they are in great
and urgent need of money.

Having, hopefully, apologised enough, let me state
my belief that for the developing world, with regard to
"globalisation", there are at least five central challenges.

The first is the most basic. It is the simple challenge
of independent thought, of thinking for ourselves. This
is not very easy, especially since there are so many kind
people who are very happy to do the thinking for us,

and who get so upset when lesser beings like us try to do our own thinking.

The second challenge is the challenge of truth. This is also not so simple because we live in a world in which there are not so many facts on globalisation and where there is so much globalisation nonsense. It is not so easy to think straight when there are so many corporate giants baring their teeth and so convincingly hiding their ambition at gobbling us all up.

The third challenge that confronts the developing world is the challenge of fairness and justice. How can we ensure a new world order that is not only new but also much fairer and much more just?

Why is it that everywhere, there is pressure to ensure "one man, one vote"? Except in the IMF and the World Bank. In these important organisations, what has to be sacred is "one dollar, one vote"?

Why is it that so much of the developed world, despite all their globalisation and liberalisation rhetoric, will not open up their agriculture market? Why do they subsidise their farmers handsomely when they declare the subsidies distort the market and the economy and all food and fuel subsidies in poor countries must be stopped or no promised loans will be disbursed?

Why is it that so many of the rich countries, despite all their globalisation and liberalisation rhetoric, will not remove the barriers on those products—textiles, clothing and footwear—in which the poor countries are world beaters? Why is there instead tariff escalation on all those important products where the developing world is able to develop awesome global competitiveness?

I believe that the fourth central challenge that faces the developing countries is the challenge of mutual benefit. How do we maximise the number of winners in the process of globalisation and minimise the number of losers? How do we ensure that we have a win-win game? How do we ensure that the results and the pattern of winners and losers is not so indefensibly skewed?

In 1960, the total income of the wealthiest 20 per cent of humanity was 30 times greater than the total income of the poorest 20 per cent. Today, after all the wonderful globalisation, it is more than 85 times greater. This figure in fact grossly understates the concentration of wealth amongst the wealthiest. The United Nations estimates that "the assets of the 200 richest people are more than the combined income of 41 per cent of the world's people." Just imagine, 200 people owning assets equal to the total wealth of 2.5 billion of their fellow creatures. How many meals a day, how many wardrobes of clothing, how many pairs of shoes, how many houses do these 200 men need in order to survive? And yet they want more and the world must accommodate them.

The globalisation theologians tell us all about "the gains from trade". Why do they not also tell us of "the pains of trade"? Why don't they tell us about the trading by a few currency traders which earn them billions at the expense of millions losing their jobs, their subsidised rice and fuel, and at times their lives? How do these many gain from trade?

It is blatantly clear that if globalisation is to proceed apace—without a war in the streets—we need a new globalisation that works less diligently in the service of the very wealthy and much harder in the service of the very poor—between nations and within nations.

I believe that the fifth central challenge is the challenge of creating a more compassionate and caring world, a world where the winner does not take all and the loser does not lose all, where much success must go to the strong and the competitive, without the weak and the uncompetitive having to descend to the depths of hell.

One of the central operating principles of globalisation is economic efficiency. The other is economic competitiveness.

In a more caring and compassionate world, all would bow to the fact that economic efficiency cannot be the be-all and end-all of every public policy. Economic efficiency, *per se*, cannot be the highest priority in all societies, at all times, under all circumstances. The idea is preposterous. If you have millions of workers jobless in a poor country, can they accept the products of the workerless automated plants in the rich countries in the interest of efficiency? Should millions starve and die in the interest of efficiency?

In a more caring and compassionate world, decent and civilised men and women must surely want to see some efficiency sacrificed in the interest of millions of poor people. The weak, the backward, the handicapped and the uncompetitive must surely also have the right to exist, to have a place in the world and to be given a helping hand. We cannot just eliminate them as Hitler tried to do with the handicapped and the mentally retarded.

Each of the five challenges I have mentioned constitutes an awesome challenge for the developing countries, which are poor, weak and un-empowered. Let me concentrate on the first two.

Let me try to stress the importance of independent thought by pointing out the danger of taking our ideas and our beliefs off the shelf. The reason is that we have so often been sold the most shoddy of products.

I cannot think of a profession more prone to being wrong than the profession of economists ... except, of course, for the profession of politicians. This, I suspect, is why they try so hard to make economics appear so complicated and mysterious, an inner sanctum to which ordinary humans (certainly people like me who have to run countries) must not go. In reality, when you take all the concocted mysteries out of it, it is clear that the economists have been hawking the most rudimentary ideas ever since our dear friend, Adam Smith, started the whole economics business in 1776.

If, fifty years ago, someone somewhere were to stand up to argue that "the market" should make the major economic and social decisions for society, that the market should discipline governments, or that the State should reduce its say in the nation, he or she would have been regarded as intellectually deficient or patently uncivilised—or both. Even the much narrower assertion that "the market" should be in charge of dictating economic policy would have been laughed out of court.

The new economic religion of our time sincerely believes that it is only right and proper, indeed it is a religious duty to believe, that the market mechanism should be allowed, in the words of an observer, to "be the sole director of the fate of human beings." It is only right and proper that "the economy" should lay down the law to society.

It is only right and proper that hedge funds and currency speculators and quick turnaround equity traders, with trillions of dollars in the bank and able to borrow many trillions more, "discipline" governments and determine the future of hundreds of millions of men, women and children whose faces they will never see, whose names they will never know. Should these young men and women come and see the mountains of humanity they throw on the rubbish heap of history as a result of their quick grab for profit and their modest quick kill? Not on your life! All they see are the figures on their computer screens moving as they depress the buttons.

How did the "lunatic fringe" move to centrestage? How did "neo-liberalism" make the transition from the intellectual ghetto to become the dominant doctrine of our time? The process by which the old economic religion has so completely given way to the new economic religion is, like the theology, the stuff of fairy tales.

The economic historians trace it to the tiny religious cell around Friedrich von Hayek and his student disciples at the University of Chicago, student disciples like Milton Friedman. From this small nucleus has sprung a huge global network of foundations, institutes, research centres, scholars, writers and public-relations hacks.

As you all know, the neo-liberal religion has many prominent temples. The IMF, the World Bank, the WTO, the most powerful amongst them, work closely with those who walk the corridors of power in the great capitals of the world, and who have such spectacular views from the skyscrapers of money on Wall Street. This once lunatic fringe who now inhabit the citadels of wealth, power and orthodoxy has huge sums of money and vast reservoirs of intellectual resources. And each year, tens of thousands more from around the world— the best and the brightest from the developing as well as the developed world—graduate from the groves of academe where the sacred truths are meticulously and lovingly taught, to swell the ranks of the priesthood.

As you know, this new economic religion has an impressive list of cardinals, the custodians of the holy writ, who develop, preserve, refine and interpret the theology. And it has developed a vast army of missionaries.

45

Think of any publication or media organisation that
we refer to as "the world media", which is supposed to
ensure the world a great diversity of views, opinions
and perspectives. Think of the TV networks: ABC,
Bloomberg, CBS, NBC, CNBC, CNN, BBC. Think of
the magazines: *Time, Newsweek, Fortune, The Economist, Far Eastern Economic Review, Asiaweek*. Think of
the newspapers: *Asian Wall Street Journal, Wall Street
Journal, Financial Times, International Herald Tribune,
The New York Times, The Washington Post, Los Angeles
Times*. I challenge you to find the world newspapers,
magazines and TV networks that are opposed to globalisation, that do not have an ideological commitment to
globalisation, that do not daily spew and propagate, directly and indirectly, explicitly and implicitly, the sacred
mantras of globalisation. I am sure there must be some.
But one would have to be extremely diligent to find one,
two, three or four in the entire world.

I am sorry to belabour this point. As you will dis-
cover in the second half of my remarks, I am not opposed to globalisation. I believe it has tremendous potentials. I know that in the case of Malaysia, several aspects of globalisation have been heaven-sent. But it is
important for all of us—not only for the humanity of the
developing world but also the humanity of the developed world—to come to their own independent judge-
ments about the dozens of facets of this complex, multi-
faceted thing we call "globalisation".

Is it not clear enough that globalisation must be an
instrument for humanity's development and not the
other way round? Surely it is not right that humanity
should be the instrument for the glory of globalisation.
Surely globalisation must not be the God whom we worship. Surely globalisation cannot be excused from cul-
pability no matter how many bones it crunches, no matter how much misery it wreaks, no matter how many fi-

nancial crises it causes, no matter how many societies it demolishes. Surely people must matter, even as profit must be secured.

Let me now proceed to the challenge of truth.

There are some who wish us to deduce truths from theology and from the sacred texts—from Adam Smith to Milton Friedman. In matters economic, I am sorry. I prefer to deduce truth from facts.

Unfortunately, the facts are not that easy to obtain, even in this mature stage of the Second Great Age of Globalisation. In part, this is because the ideology and the theology and all the globalisation hocus-pocus—on both sides of the debate—has helped to blind us.

In part, it is because we live in a world where we are up to our necks in global nonsense. It is entirely possible that 99.99 per cent of the global manufacturers of the globalisation facts have an axe to grind, a vested interest to protect, salaries to increase, a belief system to foster and intolerant Gods to satisfy. I believe that in recent times, there has been only one subject which has been propagated with greater enthusiasm and a greater disregard for the facts and for that quality which we call "wisdom". Except only for the ranting and the "dot-cons" on the so-called "dotcoms", it might be argued that never before in the history of human affairs has so much nonsense and so many lies been told in such a short time as on globalisation.

Even through the fog of the deliberate manufacturing of truths on both sides of the debate, however, some things are clear enough. It is simply not true that in the process of globalisation, all are winners. There are obviously winners and there are very obviously losers.

Second, there are winners and losers in the developing world. And there are winners and losers in the developed world. It is no accident that 58 per cent of Americans say that they are opposed to globalisation.

Third, because of differing social welfare safety nets and different levels of poverty and wealth, the immediate negative consequence of globalisation in the rich countries for most is the loss of a job. The immediate negative consequence in the impoverished countries is the termination of the practice of eating ... at least for a while. I am afraid I see no moral equivalence between a family that does not eat this weekend and a family that cannot afford to go to the movies this weekend.

I believe I am on the side of the angels when my heart goes out more to the losers in poor countries than to the losers in rich countries. Especially since there are so many, many more of them in the developing world than in the developed world. Especially since the very poor benefit so very little from some aspects of globalisation and are amongst the first and the most devastated when things go wrong.

Fourth, quite obviously, those with a lot of money have a wonderful chance of ending up the winners compared to those in the middle class who have little to play with, and compared to the poor, who have none.

Merrill Lynch and CAP Gemini Ernst & Young does a global annual survey of what they call "high net worth individuals" who have cash, stocks and other liquid assets worth at least US$1 million.

In last year's survey, Merrill Lynch and partner found that in 1999, there were slightly more than 7 million individuals who had at least US$1 million in investable liquid assets. In 1999, their total assets grew by 18 per cent, roughly US$4,000 billion, close to 5 times the total GDP of China with a population of 1.3 billion. In the latest survey published on May 14, Merrill Lynch and partner found that because of the fall in stock markets worldwide, the number of people with more than US$1 million in investable liquid assets rose by only 180,000 in the year 2000. The 7.2 million "high net worth individuals" of 2000 had a total wealth of US$27 trillion, up 6 per cent on the previous year. In the year 2000, their wealth rose by a more modest, almost paltry US$1,500 billion, not much more than 5 times the total GDP of India, with a population of a billion.

It obviously does pay to be rich in a borderless world!

I think I have said more than enough on the challenge side of the equation for developing countries. Given the stark and cruel realities, how then do we respond?

I believe that just as there are at least five central challenges that confront us, there are at least five strategic imperatives that must guide us:

- The first is the principle of rationality.
- The second is the principle of readiness.
- The third is the principle of representation.
- The fourth is the principle of responsibility.
- The fifth is the principle of self-determination.

I believe that rationality is essential because we must be careful not to throw the baby out with the bathwater. Of the dozens of dimensions of globalisation, many are indispensable for a modern economy and a modern society.

We must not turn our back on the good of globalisation, even as we must not embrace, blindly, the bad. To do so is irrational. And let us all pray to God Almighty that we all can summon the rationality and the wisdom to be able to distinguish between the good and the bad, in a world where everyone, it seems, is intent on selling us a false bill of goods.

Even when certain aspects of globalisation are productive, the problem of proper sequencing, preparation and readiness have to be seriously addressed. Nowhere has this been better demonstrated than in the great East Asian crisis of 1997 and 1998. Today, this imperative is moving to the centre of economic orthodoxy. It is being accepted even by the high priests of neo-liberalism. Most unfortunately, the neo-liberal missionaries and salesmen who, in the late 1980s and early 1990s, pressured us all to liberalise, liberalise, liberalise, forgot, in their enthusiasm, to add the proviso "when you are ready". And too many in East Asia and many other emerging markets were too starry-eyed to think it through for themselves.

Thirdly, we must ensure democracy in the processes by which the international rules and laws which are imposed on the world are discussed and adopted. It is not defensible for the rich to discuss amongst themselves in the marbled negotiating rooms in Geneva and then to present it as a *fait accompli* to the developing world. We should make it absolutely clear: No liberalisation, no globalisation without representation. The Bostonian might remember throwing tea into the sea.

Fourthly, within our own domestic jurisdictions, we must demand the highest standards of ethics, morality and sense of responsibility from the global and other corporations whose interests we seek and whose operations we host.

I believe that it is critically important for us to empower ourselves, to think for ourselves, to ensure that we have the will, the wit and the wherewithal to decide our own destiny. This is not easy in a world where the large majority of the countries of the developing world are already debt-enslaved, or under IMF rule or massive World Bank conditionalities, or are dependent on foreign aid from the developed countries. For most of these countries, who can no longer decide what they can do for their peoples, my warning, my urgings, are much too late. But as history has shown, the tide can be turned.

One of the central truths about our times is that the Second Great Age of Colonialism is already upon us. This may be fine and dandy for the perpetrators and the beneficiaries. It is not so fine and dandy for the victims and the potential victims.

For Malaysia, I say that 450 years of colonialism is enough. Malaysia must be free. We must be free to decide our future for ourselves. And we must hope that our friends, who respect freedom, will accord to us what they so naturally demand and expect for themselves.

5

The Impact of Globalisation on the Islamic World

"Muslim countries and Muslim governments have a duty to ensure that globalisation will not result in the marginalisation of their countries as happened with the Industrial Revolution and Industrial Age. We cannot afford it this time. If once again we miss this opportunity to keep pace with the radical and rapid advances now being made with technology and the sciences, and the changes they cause to the world's perceptions of things, the new ideas and concepts in human and international relations; if we miss all these and fail to handle them, then we will not only be marginalised, but be dominated and hegemonised permanently."

THIS seminar is most timely as it addresses current trends in globalisation and the challenges that it has unleashed on the developing world which, of course, include the Muslim world, for all of

A speech delivered at the International Seminar on the Impact of Globalisation on the Islamic World, in Kuala Lumpur, Malaysia, on June 11, 2001

them are developing countries, none being developed at all, although they may be very rich.

Muslims must remember that they missed the Industrial Revolution completely. While they were busy debating whether modernisation was compatible with Islam or not, while they were condemning each other over trivia regarding science and religion, while they considered for years whether electricity could be used in mosques or not, the Europeans were busy applying their new knowledge of things mechanical, of engineering, of reducing human labour with machines. They trained and reassigned their workers so as to work in factories, developed mass production techniques, constantly improved the quality of their products, reduced cost and built mass markets. They improved the speed and capacity of their transportation and captured foreign markets. And, of course, they produced better weapons and with this they put an end to the Muslim Empire. It was the Industrial Revolution which destroyed the Muslim Empire.

Now it looks like we are again going to be left behind in the Information Revolution, a revolution that will shrink the world and force Muslims to rub shoulders with all kinds of people, people not only of different religions but possessing new moral values which are totally repugnant to Muslims.

In the past we could isolate ourselves and try to practise our religion and our values free from the polluting influence of others. It is not possible today. The television and the Internet and even the telephone bring the private lives of alien people with alien cultures right into our homes, our bedrooms even. We may want to force our people to reject outside influences, we may even ban televisions and cinemas, but the question is, for how long can we do it? The invasion of our world is already on but it will become even more pervasive. There is no escaping.

Now we have globalisation, a world without borders. Can we keep out things if we have no borders? Spy planes and satellites look down at us and see everything we do. There is really no more privacy, and Muslims are very private people.

New ideas are being promoted and spread which strike at the very foundation of our religion. Can we deal with human rights which include freedom to choose one's own religion? Can we deal with the right to free access to information, including information about other religions or distorted versions of our religion and pornography?

We see the advocates of globalisation furiously preparing themselves to take advantage of a borderless world market. They are all coming together, the great banks and the giant corporations. They are acquiring and merging and acquiring and merging again. Each one of them is already bigger than most countries. They can buy up countries if they want to. Certainly they can buy our politicians.

They are truly powerful and very influential. Their governments have to do their bidding and so must other governments. Reducing investments, pulling out capital, devaluing currencies, pressuring governments to change and to legislate in their favour and a host of other things can be done by these giants which will be good for them but not necessarily good for the country in which they operate or in the world at large.

A globalised, borderless, deregulated world is what the advocates of globalisation are pushing for. How would we know when we are invaded if we have no borders? Invasion need not take the form of armies marching into our countries. We can be invaded by businessmen, by banks, by corporations, by ideas and values and moral codes which are alien to us. The effect is the same as a military invasion. In fact, it is worse than that. Every aspect of our lives will be invaded. Our minds will be invaded. Even our religion will be invaded.

I admit I am painting a frightening picture of globalisation. It is frightening but it is entirely possible, unless Muslim countries act in concert and participate in the shaping of globalisation, to redefine it, to tame it, to make it into an ideology which can benefit us as much as the rest of the world. We cannot reject globalisation outright but we can influence its interpretation, we can regulate it, we can change its pace, and we can reshape it.

Globalisation need not mean a borderless world. The borders could still be there and should be respected. With borders we can determine what can cross over and what cannot. We will not be in full control, of course. Information in all forms can cross borders unrestricted because of modern technology. But we can develop the software and even hardware which can keep out at least some of the dirt which come with the information.

With borders we can protect some of our industries until they are ready to compete. We can restrict or impose taxes on products which would compete unfairly with our businesses. We can stop the currency manipulators from impoverishing us at will, as they did in East Asia in 1997-1998. With borders there are many things we can do to sustain ourselves and to gain time to prepare for the seemingly inevitable—a totally deregulated globalisation.

There is no reason why globalisation cannot be regulated. It is nonsensical to claim that the market will regulate itself. The market is about making profits—not about ethics, not about disciplining governments. The market has shown that it is prepared for the players to fight to the death without anyone attempting to stop the fight. The market is not interested in the social consequences of maximising profits. Thus the currency traders are prepared to destroy whole economies, throw millions out of work, cause riots, arson and the killing of innocent people and the overthrow of governments, so as to make profits which are only a minute fraction of what they had destroyed.

No. The markets cannot be relied upon to regulate itself, society or governments. The regulation of the market must remain the responsibility of governments. Governments, whether democratic or not, must care for the whole nation—all the people and not just the traders. If traders have to be curbed in the greater interest of society, then the government must curb them with appropriate and adequate regulations and laws.

Monopolies and oligopolies must be broken down. Muslim countries together with other developing countries must oppose the attempts to corner the market by setting up huge banks and corporations which prevent any new business from starting up or growing. There will be a price to pay, of course. No doubt the huge and capital-rich corporations can be more efficient, reducing cost and improving quality. But we have been able to achieve a fair degree of efficiency and the quality of products have improved without these huge giant corporations or banks. The process may be slower but efficiency and quality are not static. Even with the big corporations, research and development must be continuous in order to improve results and products all the time.

On the other hand, in the absence of monopolistic giants the small can hope to build businesses independently, to innovate and to prosper reasonably. The whole world's population cannot become employees and wage-earners working for big corporations where they are just so many cogs in the numerous wheels of these giants.

Protection of local industries must be allowed, at least until they are ready to compete with the so-called multinationals. We know these multinational corporations are no more multinational than are our industries. Their labour force may be from many nations but their ownership and their direction remains with the very rich countries.

The pace of globalisation must be slowed now. It is advancing too rapidly. The developing countries are unable to cope even with the negotiations on world trade. Against the numerous experts from the rich countries, their negotiating teams can make no headway. Divided, the developing countries including the Muslim countries are no match for the sophisticated arguments of the experts representing the rich advocates of globalisation.

Currency trading should be regulated and totally transparent if at all there should be currency trading. Currency is not a commodity which can be used as raw material or for consumption. Currency is mere tokens and their values are entirely artificial. Governments are the only authority which can assign values to the currency. Of course, governments can cause currencies to devalue by mismanagement but it is entirely possible for governments to fix the exchange rate of the currencies. An international organisation can be created which will determine whether there should be a change in the exchange rate or not. Many things can be done with the international financial regime which can stabilise exchange rate and free international trade from uncertain exchange rates.

These are some of the things that can be done to render globalisation less dangerous to the developing countries. There are probably many more modifications which can be made to globalisation in order to ensure that it will benefit everyone, rich and poor, big and small, developed and developing.

But while we try to change or to stall globalisation, we cannot afford to wait for the results of our actions. We must be prepared to deal with the dangers posed by globalisation and we must learn all about the technologies and the applications they can offer. We cannot afford the kind of suspicions we had entertained about industrialisation and modernisation this time round. Of course, there will still be those who would say that worldly success is not for us Muslims. For us the afterlife is more important. If disaster strikes us the Almighty will save us for we are Muslims.

Those who say this forget that Allah will not change the fate of those who do not strive to change their fate themselves. If we just make no attempt to handle the threat posed by globalisation, if we simply leave it to Allah's will, we really cannot expect the Almighty to save us.

Unfortunately, there are many Muslims in these countries and I believe in most other Muslim countries who will not only do nothing to save themselves but who will actually actively try to prevent other Muslims from taking any pre emptive action by violently opposing it. Since they consider that we should leave our fate in the hands of Allah, it is strange that they should actually be taking positive steps to prevent Muslims from saving themselves. They should leave it to Allah to stop us. But when it comes to propagating their belief they are prepared to act and they don't trust Allah to do it for them. But whether it is strange or not every time Muslim countries try to take positive measures to keep up with development in the rest of the world and to prevent themselves from being dominated by others, there will be groups of Muslim fanatics who will do their best (or worst) to keep Muslims backwards and vulnerable in the name of Islam. In fact these Muslims who want us to remain backward are traitors to Islam and the Muslims. Knowingly or unknowingly they are working for the enemies of Islam.

And so if we the majority of the Muslims want to avoid being swallowed up by globalisation we must learn to master it. The first things that Muslim countries must do is to learn all about information technology which is so intricately linked to globalisation.

Learning about information technology should not be confined to its application alone. We must have the capacity to develop the basic software which is so very essential and yet so very costly for us to acquire now. We must develop our own basic software on which to develop other softwares. We must in fact develop our own Internet or Intranet. There is no reason at all why we must use only the Internet for all applications.

This is a tall order perhaps but what some people can do others can also do. And we should be able to do better.

Beyond software we must develop our own hardware. We must design and produce the microchips without which there would be no information technology. We must develop all kinds of applications for the microprocessors, applications not only in computers and communication but also in engineering, in automated machines and robots, in precision engineering, in the manufacture of sophisticated instruments and appliances and a host of other applications.

From these we must develop our own manufacturing industries so as to reduce our dependence on others. In fact, we must now catch up with the Industrial Revolution that we missed. Our manufacturing capacity must at least be equal to those of developed countries.

Perhaps this thing that I propose is a tall dream. It is, of course, a dream. But we do have the resources and the expertise, albeit limited at the moment. We are not going to beat the developed countries but we should be able to catch up with them in time, or at least not be left so far behind as we are now.

We have a duty to our religion to do this. Globalisation is not just about material wealth but also about values. We see the destruction of morality in the materialistic world. Today, homosexuality is actively encouraged and in some instances even incestuous relation between siblings and parents and children are tolerated. It seems that in the name of human rights anything is allowed, nothing is barred. Marriage and families are no longer respected institutions. They are neither formalised nor considered necessary. Families are defined as two people or more living together without any recognised marriage ceremony or registration and begetting and rearing children of indeterminate parentage.

Muslim countries and Muslim governments have a duty to ensure that globalisation will not result in the marginalisation of their countries as happened with the Industrial Revolution and Industrial age. We cannot afford it this time. If once again we miss this opportunity to keep pace with the radical and rapid advances now being made with technology and the sciences, and the changes they cause to the world's perceptions of things, the new ideas and concepts in human and international relations; if we miss all these and fail to handle them, then we will not only be marginalised, but be dominated and hegemonised permanently.

We also stand exposed to the undermining of our religion and our value system. We may think we can isolate and insulate ourselves but this is a false hope. Even if we can keep our borders, we cannot prevent wireless communication from penetrating our society.

Already we have to accept and practise alien ideologies, concepts and values. Our systems of government have to change and we have to constantly justify and apologise for our practices and values. Of course, some of us are extreme and we should condemn them but the vast majority of us are moderate and rational. Our systems and our values are not absolutely bad although we have to rid ourselves of pre-Islamic and cultural values which are actually not Islamic but tribal.

We the moderates and the rational must try to understand globalisation, the technology that is driving it and the inevitability of globalisation in some form or another. Understanding this we must prepare ourselves not only to fend off the dangers but to make use of globalisation so as to catch up with the developed countries in both information technology and industrial capacity. We must not miss this opportunity if we want to preserve our independence and the essence of our religion and values. Whether the impact of globalisation on us will be beneficial or not depends upon us. Blaming others will get us nowhere. Remember the Quranic injunction that Allah will not change the fate of those who do not try to improve their fate themselves. Remember also that all that is bad is due to our own doing, all that is good comes from Allah.

6

Beyond Globalism and Globalisation

"So what is there beyond globalism and globalisation?
There could be total oppression of the weak by the
strong as capitalism runs riot. Or there could be a world
democracy where the resources of the world are
combined with human ingenuity to create the greatest
human civilisation ever."

PERHAPS it is too much to expect
to foresee what will the situation be in the world beyond
globalisation, considering that we are only just into globalisation and we are not only unable to fully comprehend it but quite obviously we are making a mess of it.

A speech delivered at the 7th International Conference on the
Future of Asia in Tokyo, Japan, on June 8, 2001

Only a few years back we were all opening our arms to welcome globalisation. We had become a global village. Modern technology had enabled instant communication, instant sound and sights across the vastness of continents. We could actually commute almost halfway across the world for a breakfast meeting and still be back home for dinner with our families.

No country could isolate or insulate itself. Privacy, even of individuals was becoming more and more difficult. Prying eyes looked down on us from outer space or sometimes from much lower down. A global village is really smaller than an ordinary village in terms of visibility for it is quite roofless.

There is no doubt about the benefits of unlimited communication. We can be lost in the ocean or the desert and yet be able to talk to people and indicate our position through the magic of cellular telephony. We can see things even as they happen on the other side of the world.

We know a lot more about our environment and the danger it is faced with. And we know how we can preserve it. We know of the species which are about to be extinct and our need to save them. The regions which we once considered as hostile to Man, which we avoided or tried to eliminate before, we now wish to preserve and we can pour in billions for the preservation of these places.

Technology advanced, is advancing and will advance ever more rapidly. There is nothing that technology cannot do. If an animal, a fish or a plant is not big enough, we can double their sizes and their food contents. The genetically modified salmon is three times bigger, the vegetable greener and nutritious and cattle yield the exact combination of fat and protein and carbohydrate to suit our tastebuds, and perhaps our health.

We humans can do anything. We merely have to decide what we want and somewhere in the world there will be scientists who will produce it for us. We don't have to give birth to babies anymore, we can clone them. Why should anyone give birth naturally and painfully or even by caesarean section? Why not produce perfect replicas of ourselves with all the characteristics we like best?

We can reach the moon and the stars. So far we have found them uninhabited, but should there be any creature out there with the audacity to challenge us, we will blast them into nothingness with our ray guns. What a glorious future for the arms makers. We will all have to buy laser guns to blast the Martians and the Venusians into empty space. We will fight terrestrial wars too, for we cannot give up our addiction to it. We are busy inventing and producing ever newer weapons which we must try out in real life. How else can we know whether they work or not.

Well, this could be the post-globalisation scenario. But I hope and pray that this will not be. And this will not be only if we take a grip of ourselves and refuse to become the captives of mad scientists and their fantastic technologies. Simply because we can do something, simply because we can now play God, does not mean we should play God. We can, if we want to, destroy humanity completely. Between Russia and the US there are enough nuclear warheads to pulverise the whole planet. But we won't do it because we know that truly will be the end of history.

Similarly we will not clone ourselves. We will not do it because we cannot interfere too much with God's work, which others prefer to call nature. Look at what happened when they imported rabbits into Australia and then they brought European dogs to kill the rabbits.

We are more concerned now about preserving the trees and the forests, and the animals. But we go too far sometimes. We deny the poor in the world living space for themselves because we want their countries to become carbon sinks. Yet the protected animals are allowed to destroy the forests and even kill and eat humans. The man being eaten by the tiger must appreciate that he is helping to preserve an endangered species.

We are more civilised now but the lunatic fringe keeps pushing us to go too far. We are going too far with our globalisation also. We want globalisation to be totally unregulated, to be left to the markets to govern it. But the market is about making profits, maximising profits. In the process it is likely to leave a trail of disasters and tragedies. But never mind, the important thing is that globalisation must be accompanied by market deregulation. As long as the global marketplace is deregulated what happens to people does not matter. The system has become more important than the people it is supposed to serve.

Remember socialism and communism? They were all responses and reactions to the inequities and the oppressions in human societies. The great thinkers of the time believed that if men were made absolutely equal, then they would enjoy a life free of oppression, free of envy, free of conflicts and of war. They believed that all that man wanted was to be equal and free. They invented the slogan *"Liberté, Egalité, Fraternité"* and made a religion of it.

But egalitarianism led instead to oppressive dictatorships; the massacres of millions in order to achieve equality, freedom and the brotherhood of men. For many who did not take kindly to the ideology there was no liberty and no fraternity. There was only oppression and death.

In the end these great dreams, these ideologies were recognised for what they were, the cause of further sufferings and the deaths of millions. And they were discarded.

Democracy too will go this way, not because it is a bad system but because it keeps on being reinterpreted and embellished. At first democracy was only about majority rule. Then minority rights was added, then individual rights. These rights were constantly being broadened so that in the end they became more important than majority rights. The government may be elected by the majority but minorities may bring it down by street violence helped by the media and even foreign interests. The rule of law is advocated but this simply means that those opposed to the government may break the law but the government may not enforce the law against them.

Then along came the non-governmental organisations to claim the right to frustrate popularly elected governments. They may be made up of only one person but they get wide publicity and support; they may use illegal means. They can become extremely powerful and frequently governments of the majority have to bow to them.

Democracy is now no longer about the rule of the majority. Indeed in many cases the elections to gain majority support is an exercise in futility. For promptly the popularly elected government is hamstrung and rendered impotent. The wishes of the majority, the largely silent majority, is ignored while the governments struggle to placate the activist minority.

Now the minority has become more violent and lawfully elected governments have been toppled by the illegal activities of the few, the street mobs. In the meantime the country becomes unstable, unable to develop

67

and for many developing countries, their freedom is lost. The people suffer, as law and order breaks down, ethnic and religious clashes escalate, and thousands are killed. Mob rule has become more democratic than majority rule.

Democracy has been abused until everything can be done in the name of democracy. The better life promised has not materialised. Instead people are suffering more than ever, more even than when they had authoritarian rule, because of democracy. The time will surely come when democracy will go the way of socialism and communism. It is not because democracy is bad. It is still the best system of governance. But democracy has been so abused that it no longer is able to benefit either the majority or the minority.

Today democracy still reigns supreme. To criticise it is to be heretical and to expose oneself to vilification. But eventually the damage will be so evident and so great that democracy will become a bad word just as proletarian dictatorship is a bad word, and it will be rejected.

But this need not happen. Democracy can be saved if it is not regarded as perfect, if its weaknesses and defects are recognised and remedies made and excesses curbed.

And now we have globalisation, a great idea whose time has come. But already it has started on the wrong footing. Currency manipulations across borders and the economic and financial catastrophes such as those in Orange County, in Brazil, in Mexico, in Russia, and, of course, in East Asia, which followed this particular manifestation of globalisation do not augur well for the future of globalisation. The victims are told it is free trade and therefore it must be good.

But must we have horrendous disasters as a price for globalisation? Is globalisation without the pain, unbearable pain, possible? The answer is, yes. Globalisation need not be accompanied by total deregulation. The two are not the same. Some regulations can make globalisation not only less destructive but also beneficial all round.

The assumption that markets will regulate themselves is contrary to logic or human nature. The market is about maximising profits. It is not a social organisation intended to cure social ills. It is not even about fairness, justice and good governance.

The market, especially the free market, operates by defeating competition. To do this well the players must be strong and ruthless. And so we see the mergers of the giants and the mergers of the merged giants. The idea is to be so big and therefore so strong that competition would be one-sided. The smaller groups will either lose and be destroyed, resulting in terrible social and economic damage or they can submit to being taken over. Eventually there can be only one player in one industry. Then competition would cease and the winner will become an arrogant and domineering entity, optimising profits at the expense of quality, efficiency and social considerations.

The world will be badly served by the monopolistic giants, which may gang up in order to be even more powerful. Governments will not be able to control them because governments will depend entirely on them. In fact, they will determine who the government will be. Their control will now become absolute. Big Brother, big capital, will rule the world and the poor and the weak will just have to submit.

Oligopolies and monopolies need not be an essential feature of globalisation. There could be statutory limits to mergers and the size of corporations. In any business a sufficiently large number of players must be ensured. Competition must be governed by a set of rules to ensure not just a level playing field but the contestants are fairly evenly matched. There must be banks and businesses which are national and those which are international. The weak must be protected according to a set of internationally agreed rules.

An international currency should be created which belongs to no one country. Rates of exchange should be based on this one currency which can be used for payment of all international trade. Earnings in this currency must be immediately deposited with a nation's central bank, and local currency issued for local transactions. The reserves must be held in this international currency only and not a basket of currencies.

Currencies must never be traded as commodities. Should there be a need to devalue against the international currency, a panel of central banks and the international bank should determine the proper exchange rate. No country should dominate international finance and commerce.

If we are prepared to be pragmatic and fair, if we are ready to curb the excesses of democracy and globalisation and to determine the right levels that will be suitable and acceptable in any particular country, if we are prepared to give up the idea of being dominant because we are the richest and the most powerful, then we can look with hope beyond globalisation.

Globalisation today ignores the very poor. In a globalised world wealth distribution should be equally global. But it is not.

The world of today is extremely rich. A combination of technologies and natural resources have made unlimited wealth creation possible. There is more than enough wealth to wipe out global poverty completely.

The financial system of a globalised world is now confined to a free flow of capital. Those who profit from such flows must be prepared to pay a global levy. The levy should be based on the GDP of nations.

Voluntary aid to the poor is now anathema to the rich. The levy should be for statutory aid. It should be for the building of needed infrastructures such as roads, canals, railroads, ports, airports, power and water to stimulate growth.

The levy should be administered by an international agency, including the construction of the infrastructure by international constructors. Subcontracts and supplies should come from the locals. The benefits would obviously be evenly distributed. The infrastructure built will enable products to be exported and imported at lower cost. World trade will certainly grow and poverty eradicated.

Altogether the levy would be a win-win formula. No one will lose. The whole world will be enriched. The poor countries will be less poor and will truly become a part of the globalised world. Globalisation would then be meaningful as it involves the whole world.

Of course, the rich will not take kindly to this idea. But if they expect that the poor should always accept ideas which benefit the rich, then the rich should also be prepared to accept ideas which benefit the poor, especially when the rich will benefit as well.

Even as in a country the poor have a right to some of the wealth of the country, a globalised world must accord the poor similar rights. If the poor cannot expect this then why should they accept globalisation?

So what is there beyond globalism and globalisation? There could be total oppression of the weak by the strong as capitalism runs riot. Or there could be a world democracy where the resources of the world are combined with human ingenuity to create the greatest human civilisation ever.

7

Countering Negative Aspects of Globalisation through Smart Partnership

"Smart partnership can help unify concerns and to formulate a common stand and embark on cooperative actions in order to counter any perceived negative forces of globalisation affecting the emerging economies."

LET us be reminded that globalisation is not merely a process but has also become an ideology. From one international forum to another, the proponents of unbridled, supposedly "unstoppable" forces of globalisation and trade liberalisation continue to sing their song of "the ticket to a better life for every-

A speech delivered at the meeting on Global 2000 International Smart Partnership in Maputo, Mozambique, on August 21, 2000

one ". This ideology is preached to us as being full of glorious benefits. I continue to look long and hard for evidence that this may, in fact, be true. But all around, the arrows point in the opposite direction. Sadly, the number of downturns and negative aspects of globalisation which many of us have actually experienced are seldom mentioned or discussed. If they are, they are not attributed to globalisation but to things like bad governance, lack of democracy, cronyism, etc.

In nation building, when caution is not exercised and care not taken; when the interest of people and nations are gambled upon on the basis of an "ideology", when decisions are not grounded in reality and the hard facts are ignored, there will be calamity. The promoters of the ideologies are to blame, of course. But we who make the decision to convert cannot be totally blameless. How many times have we seen ideologies destroy nations and yet when a new ideology is promoted we accept it as the perfect and infallible solution to all our problems.

The man in the street may be oblivious to the forces of globalisation. Yet it will affect him with as much intensity, as it will the heads of government and captains of industries. The reactions of governments and industries to globalisation will bear finally on the ability of individuals to enjoy economic freedom and empowerment; and whether individuals live in a free land and be master of their own destiny. Globalisation merits serious thinking and we need to strategise our responses to the major issues ranging from business globalisation and trade liberalisation, sustainable development, the knowledge-driven economy and the sociopolitical concerns such as democracy, the rule of law and human rights.

If the amount of money circulating around the globe is anything to go by, we are trading more now than at any other moment in human history. Financial liberalisation has certainly been extensive, and the world has borne witness to massive financial flows and market penetrations. The volume traded in the world foreign exchange market has grown from a daily average of US$15 billion in 1973, to over US$900 billion in 1992, and the number today far exceeds US$1,000 billion a day.

But where does all this money go? What productive and essential economic activities does it support? The hard reality is that a mere 2 per cent of foreign exchange traded is used for trade payments. The rest of the transactions are all speculative in nature. And speculation is non-productive. In fact, it is truly destructive, as the East Asian economies learnt to their detriment during the 1997-1998 financial and economic turmoil.

Who benefits from all of these so called trade liberalisation'? The beneficiaries are clearly a select and privileged group. The top five of the world's population in the richest countries enjoy 82 per cent of the expanding export trade and 68 per cent of FDI—the bottom five barely more than one per cent. Between 1980 and 1996 only 33 countries managed to sustain 3 per cent annual growth. For 59 countries mainly in sub-Saharan Africa and Eastern Europe and the CIS, GNP per capita had, in fact, declined.

Twenty per cent of the world's population in the developed countries receive 82.7 per cent of the total world income, while the 20 per cent of the world's population in the poorest countries receive only 1.4 per cent. In 1989 the average income of the 20 per cent of people living in the richest countries was 60 times higher than that of the 20 per cent living in the poorest countries. What is more alarming is that this ratio has doubled, from 30 times in 1950.

The glorious promises of globalisation have yet to materialise. A reckless approach to trade liberalisation without due consideration for one's own ability to cope will only contribute to a vicious cycle of trade and balance of payments deficits, financial instability, debt and recession, not to mention the social costs of dumping and general economic erosion.

A misstep carries with it a cost no less than catastrophic for nations and people. A blind acceptance of an ideology that to date stands as just that—an ideology—is unacceptable, naive and downright dangerous.

To equate globalisation with a guarantee for economic advancement is a gross oversimplification of the realities that surround international trade. Despite the best of intentions and the most progressive macroeconomic policies of developing nations, better trade performance does not necessarily translate into increases in living standards. Given the international division of labour, where high-priced goods are produced by the advanced nations of the world, and the production of low-value items are relegated to developing nations, the terms of trade for developing countries are almost always unfavourable.

I am not convinced that the developed nations are at all interested in this so-called "level playing field". Globalisation as it stands clearly means access of products of developed nations into the developing world. And yet, high tariffs still persist in developed countries in sectors such as agriculture, textiles and steel in which developing countries may have comparative advantage. If not tariffs, then it is standards, subsidies, labour conditions, human rights—the goalposts keep changing against our favour.

This clearly calls for a new way of thinking, for developing nations to chart a new paradigm in nation building such that old mistakes are not repeated. Given the onslaught of voices propagating the good of an open and liberal economy, sovereignty as a basis for self-determination and empowerment seems contradictory and out of place. Yet at no time is it more relevant than it is now.

It is not without a good reason that the last WTO round in Seattle came to a stalemate. Nation building is not only about the lowest cost, it is equally about social justice and a conducive environment for the development of human dignity. A grain of rice, wheat, maize or barley is not simply an issue of how much it cost to produce but does the person planting it make a decent living? And who ends up eating the produce? Nation building is about the ability and freedom and flexibility to make strategic choices in finance, trade and investment for oneself. If nations are willing to accept higher prices in order to acquire the technologies to compete later, that should be the right of sovereign nations to decide.

It is ironic that the very same people who advocate freedom of speech and rights of expression are the very same to clamp down hard on what they see as dissenting views on their brand of globalisation. Malaysia's rejection of the IMF formula and the decision to regain exchange rate control and regulate the flows of short-term capital have now been reluctantly accepted by the international community as a viable alternative to the IMF prescription. By their own admission, a "cure all" for economic ills of the world simply does not exist. Yet barely are we out of the crisis, a new "prescription" is being forced down our throats. How soon we forget. And what is the price of such a memory lapse?

Developing nations must ask themselves where do they want to go from here. What are the options open to them and what they intend to do about it. While the developed world embraces the new knowledge-driven ᴊ economy in all eagerness, developing economies, to the level that is comfortable and attainable, must also embark on a quest for knowledge in all its forms.

Knowledge is the domain of all the citizens of the world and cuts across all strata of economic activity. It is certainly not limited to cutting edge technology and the ICT sector, as we are commonly led to believe.

It is on this premise that Malaysia has embarked on an agenda for intensification of knowledge use in all sectors of the economy, new and traditional. This entails the concerted effort of all stakeholders in the Malaysian economy to acquire and generate bodies of knowledge. Coupled with the ability to effectively translate knowledge into technological and social advancement that elevates the living standards of the populace, this is empowerment in its truest sense.

Technology-based economic development is a unique phenomenon. Development was once a matter of accumulating physical and human capital. Within that process there is what is known as the "convergence factor". This assumes that a well-governed developing country experiences high returns from investment, which in turn attracts an inflow of foreign capital, thus narrowing the gap between rich and poor nations.

Technological advancement, however, dances to a different tune. With increasing returns to scale in their favour, regions with advanced technologies are best placed to further innovate, with the gap between the technological haves and have-nots ever widening. Innovation requires physical, financial and social infrastructure—demanding even to the most advanced of nations. But a developing country grappling with limited resources and a multitude of needs will fail to innovate. Worse still, whatever talents they may have would be enticed away because they lack the facilities and could not match the terms offered by rich countries.

Emerging economies, therefore, must see the process of globalisation from all aspects. Most decision making at the international level seemed to safeguard the interests of the more matured economies without regard to national sovereignty, economic freedom, economic empowerment, socioeconomic programmes, and technology development agenda being undertaken by developing nations.

It is precisely in this context that the smart partnership practice promises to make the most impact. Smart partnership can help unify concerns and actions and to formulate a common stand and embark on cooperative actions in order to counter any perceived negative forces of globalisation affecting the emerging economies. The smart partnership dialogues, such as this, can well serve as focal points to deliberate and share our views and experiences and to nurture continued interactions among members and smart partners in between dialogues.

I observe that CPTM, the Commonwealth Partnership for Technology Management, can assume a catalytic role in synergising the many different dimensions of the subject of globalisation with a truly achievable "win-win" result. "National smart partnership hubs" will have to come forward, and work closely with CPTM, and set priorities for action. In this regard, I would like to offer MIGHT, the 'Malaysian smart partnership hub' to assist whenever we can.

8

Let South Nations Have a Role in Shaping Globalisation

"Globalisation has already shown signs of becoming a religion that tolerates no heresy. This is rather unfortunate, for globalisation, if properly interpreted and regulated, can bring about a great deal of wealth and benefit to the world, the rich as well as the poor. The important thing is to focus on the results rather than dogma."

OUR gathering here today may be regarded as a manifestation of our unity and solidarity. However, while it is easy to meet it is not so easy to act together. Therein lies our weakness.

The rich are apparently more united. Theirs is a small group of only seven countries. Although they may

A speech delivered at The South Summit in Havana, Cuba, on April 12, 2000

have varying degrees of differences between them, they close rank very rapidly if their dominance is challenged.

Their approach is very simple. Should there be any new ideas in the social, economic or political field they would quickly come up with their own interpretations, which are designed to benefit them. Thus we see them foisting on the world their moral values, their political systems and now economic globalisation. The South has no choice but to react to their interpretations. And reacting limits the choice and is less beneficial.

Presently the focus is on globalisation. Technological advances is the excuse for doing away with the independence of nations and replacing it with interdependent nations. We are told through their propaganda machines that globalisation is an idea whose time has come and resistance would be futile.

We had welcomed globalisation believing that foreign capital, know-how, etc, could help our economies to grow. Then in East Asia the rogue currency traders demonstrated that simply by devaluing our currencies they can make the so-called East Asian economic tigers suddenly into meowing cats. Millions were thrown out of work and made destitute. The international institutions then moved in ostensibly to help with loans but in reality to facilitate the takeover of the countries' economy and even politics.

All these are made possible because the rich interprets globalisation as the right of capital to cross and re-cross borders at will. Capital is the new gunship of the rich. By coming in with short-term investments they create an illusion of wealth. Once that has happened they merely have to pull out their capital in order to impoverish and weaken their victims and force them to submit to foreign dictates.

But if globalisation implies integration of all countries into one single global entity then why should it mean only the free flow of capital and capitalists across borders? Why should not workers, especially unemployed ones, move across borders freely? If money is capital for the rich, labour is the capital of the poor countries. They should be allowed to migrate to the rich countries, to compete for the jobs there just as the powerful corporations of the rich must be allowed to compete with their tiny counterparts in the poorer countries. Just as the big corporations from the rich can easily put out of business the small companies of the poor, the hardworking lower-paid workers of the poor can easily displace the high-cost labour in the rich countries. The result would be lower production cost and lower cost of living for the rich and more remittances to poor countries.

This is a ridiculous idea, of course. How can one expect a rich country to let poor people in to displace their highly paid workers? But if it is right for the big corporations of the rich to displace small weak corporations of the poor, why is it so wrong for the poor workers to displace the rich workers in the rich countries?

The economic turmoil in East Asia has resulted in the rich taking what belongs to the poor. As the banks and businesses of the former Asian tigers collapse and as their share prices plunge, the rich have moved in to buy the devalued shares and acquire the companies. They could have bought at normal prices during normal times but they preferred to emasculate us before they take over at a fraction of the cost. Backing this move are the international institutions, which insist that we open up our countries so that the predators can move in to take over everything. Governments may not protect local businesses. Market forces must prevail and since money equals force in the market, those with money will dominate.

We admit that we are not perfect. We have corruption, cronyism, etc. But so have the rich. Despite our alleged corruption, etc we had developed our countries and given our people a good life. The market forces, which want to eliminate corruption, etc in our countries have had no noticeable success despite the high cost to us. But they have certainly made fortunes by their manipulations of the currencies and the market and now by their acquisition of the banks, industries and businesses.

Globalisation should stress results rather than methods. Presently we are being told that globalisation must be espoused and practised even if it destroys us.

We are falling into the old trap of believing that systems on their own can solve human problems. When we put too much faith in a system we will forget the reasons why the system was initially formulated. Systems are devised because they are believed to be able to right current wrongs and bring benefits to the practitioners. Unfortunately once a system is accepted, it becomes so sacred that even if the results it delivers are worse than the situation it was supposed to remedy, it must still be upheld, defended and practised. At that stage if anyone dares to go against the system he will be regarded as a heretic and universally condemned.

Globalisation has already shown signs of becoming a religion that tolerates no heresy. This is rather unfortunate, for globalisation, if properly interpreted and regulated, can bring about a great deal of wealth and benefit to the world, the rich as well as the poor. The important thing is to focus on the results rather than dogma. If the results are good then by all means implement it as currently interpreted and practised, but if the results are bad for anyone, then globalisation must be reinterpreted and modified until the expected results are achieved.

It is a mistake to exclude the weak and the poor from participating in the formulation of globalisation. They have a great deal of experience. We have seen in the East how foreign direct investment (FDI), technological transfers and opening up of the markets of the rich has resulted in the poor countries becoming enriched. We have also seen how nations can be made poor suddenly. Our experience can help shape a globalisation that benefits all. So let us in.

There is no doubt that if globalisation is properly interpreted and practised it can result in a more equitable world order where wealth is more evenly distributed between the rich and the poor. Badly interpreted it can destroy the poor especially and by extension stifle the growth of the rich.

This is a summit of the countries of the South. There are many of us and each one of us is poor and unable to influence international policies in our favour. But weak though each one of us may be, our combined strength is very considerable. It is therefore imperative that we act together if we want to be effective.

Today, political or ideological interests are of less importance than economic growth and greater material wealth for our people. Most of us believe that free trade and private investments can help achieve these. We believe that globalisation can contribute to more rapid growth through the free flow of goods, services and capital. But we also know that the best-run economies can run into deep trouble. We the poorer countries cannot afford the recessions. We believe we can contribute towards avoiding recessions. Therefore our views should be taken seriously in the formulation of the international financial and economic systems.

9

A New Globalisation in a New World Order

"It is time to have a new globalisation that works less in the service of the very wealthy and much harder in the service of the very poor. It is time for us to ensure that development is brought to the very centre of the global agenda as our principal objective."

ALMOST ten years ago, in the euphoria that gripped many parts of "the Western world" immediately after the Gulf War, a president of a great, powerful and triumphant nation by the name of George Bush made a historic speech at Maxwell Air Force Base in Montgomery, Alabama, calling for a "New

A speech delivered at a Conference in Kuala Lumpur, Malaysia, on February 26, 2001

World Order". This was a man who had repeatedly
called for a "kinder, gentler America". His son is now
President. The new Bush talks of unity and solidarity
and of compassionate conservatism for the United
States. I am sure many will wish him every success in
his mission.

This morning, allow a simple Prime Minister from
this small country in what some still call "the Far East"
to make a simple speech in his capital of Kuala Lumpur
also calling for "A New World Order". Let me also make
a simple plea for a world order that is not only new but
one that is much more just, much more productive—a
kinder, gentler world order that is a lot more caring, a
great deal more compassionate.

Such a New World Order must care a great deal for
ethics and morality, for liberty and independence, for
equality and mutual respect, and for productive democracy and comprehensive human rights. Comprehensive
human rights, amongst which the right to human dignity, to work and the right to put food on the family table
are as basic and fundamental as any other.

Let me make a passionate plea for the unity not of a
segment of humanity but for all of mankind; for compassionate widespread developmentalism, for the development and prosperity of all the children of Adam—for
not only the strong, the rich and the incredibly empowered who should survive and thrive in the fiercely competitive global jungle but also for the disadvantaged, the
poor and the miserably disenfranchised who cannot.

Let me make a passionate plea for a new globalisation in a New World Order.

The new globalisation that we must foster must
rightly reward enterprise and excellence; but it must
contribute to and not detract from this more just, more

caring, kinder, gentler, more compassionate New World Order.

The new globalisation that we must foster must contribute to and not detract from greater ethics and morality, greater liberty and independence, greater equality and mutual respect, greater productive democracy and comprehensive human rights.

What do I mean by justice? It is not the hallowed and civilised principle of "special and differential", for a temporary privilege to be afforded to the especially weak and vulnerable, that was the hallmark of the global system for so long. Today, most of us do not even dare to mention "special and differential". Today, all that we ask for, is plain old simple fair play.

Even the IMF says that the developed countries impose the highest trade barriers on the manufactured goods in which the developed countries have the greatest comparative advantage. These manufactured goods are textiles, clothing and footwear. Is this fair?

When the developing world goes to the WTO and asks for trade liberalisation on textiles, on clothing and footwear, it is out-stonewalled and it is told that this is simply not do-able. The political costs to the governments of the rich which have to get elected are simply too high. Is this fair? Is this just?

Poor developing countries must move heaven and earth to liberalise. In fact, when they are under the thumb of the IMF, they have very little choice but to move heaven and earth, no matter the merciless consequences on their people and their societies.

Health services must be terminated. Medicines must be dispensed with. Schools should be closed. Children should stop going to them. Huge masses of people should be thrown out of work. And food and fuel be priced beyond the reach of most people. What are these things? Merely what the IMF and the well-tutored economists call "structural adjustment". But for the rich and powerful, even the most marginal concessions on textiles, clothing and footwear are not possible. For that matter, for most of the rich, the most basic fair play on agriculture, the hope of the non-industrialised developing world, is also politically un-doable.

Bill Clinton recently made a speech, one of his last as President of the United States, at the University of Warwick, where he spoke passionately, with wit and a heavy dose of civility, on globalisation. Clinton was on the side of the angels when he noted: "If the wealthiest countries ended our agricultural subsidies, levelling the playing field for the world's farmers, that alone could increase the income of developing countries by US$20 billion a year." So why not do it? Why not remove the subsidies? Why not play fair? Why not level the playing field? Why not give the hundreds of millions of farmers in the developing world a better chance to put food in the mouths of their children and a few cents in their pocket?

Clinton, a great champion of globalisation himself, gave the following answer. It is "not as simple as it sounds," Clinton says. "I see these beautiful fields in Great Britain; I have driven down the highways of France; I know there is a cultural social value to the fabric that has developed here over the centuries." Indeed.

Perhaps the point has also to be made with equal force and passion that putting food in the mouths of one's children and a few cents into one's pocket is also of some "cultural social value". Perhaps it may even be arguable that this could be of a higher human value than the beauty of manicured agricultural fields, which can be admired by all motorists driving down the highways of Europe—especially since the luxury of this great "cultural social value" can be secured in other ways, not at the cost of impoverished farmers in the poor developing world.

So much for justice. How about caring and compassion, and a more productive globalisation, focused on development, in a kinder and gentler world?

The market fundamentalists and the globalisation theologians have elevated what they call "survival of the fittest" and "economic efficiency", the maximisation of profits, the making of money as the most important moral basis of their religion. All too often survival of the fittest merely means survival of those with the least scruples. It certainly does not mean survival of the best or the most worthy.

We must throw off the intellectual hegemony of the globalisation theologians. It is time to put people before profit, to ensure that in the process of globalisation there are many more winners and many fewer losers.

It is time to have a new globalisation that works less in the service of the very wealthy and much harder in the service of the very poor. It is time for us to ensure that development is brought to the very centre of the global agenda as our principal objective.

It is time to put our mental house in order, to distinguish between means and ends, to make sure that everyone understands that trade and investment liberalisation, marketisation and competitiveness, the entire WTO agenda, are means to the ultimate end of human development.

Some may refer to my aversion to gobbledygook, globaloney and gobble-isation—indeed, to all I have said—as a return to basics. I prefer to see it as an attempt to move forward to the fundamentals.

I do realise that this new globalisation in a New World Order that I advocate is a new paradigm. It is a strange intellectual universe compared to the dog-eat-dog world and the law of the jungle that the globalisation theologians of this day are committed to. The fact that this is so, the fact that they will oppose and discredit this new paradigm should fortify us in our conviction and in our commitment.

We must make absolutely sure that we will not swallow the absolute market fundamentalism that the globalisation extremists try to ram down our throats, that the absolute capitalism that the globalisation extremists want to unleash on this planet will not run riot, that the absolute globalisation that the globalisation extremists want to impose on the entire world will not come to pass.

Please do not get me wrong. I do not advocate abandonment of the market system. I do not advocate the rejection of capitalism. I do not advocate opposition to globalisation.

I must confess to being a believer in the market system. I am a believer in the capitalist system. I am also a believer in globalisation. You don't have to watch my lips. You don't have to examine the words I use. You merely have to look around you at the Malaysia that exists today.

Ever since we imposed selective currency controls on September 1, 1998, the so-called world media and the high priests of globalisation have been accusing this country of turning its back on the world. The so-called world media daily refers to my "xenophobic diatribes" my antics. No doubt, my speech today will also be described as a "xenophobic diatribe" designed to justify putting my former deputy in jail. Let me merely state a simple fact: Malaysia today is amongst the halfdozen most globalised and open countries in the world.

This did not happen in an extended fit of forgetfulness. It did not happen by accident. The world did not descend on us. We had to grab the world by the throat to bring them to us. We had to work tirelessly. The fact that we are such an open economy and such an open society is the result of deliberate policy, consistent determination and an ocean of toil, tears and sweat. We are not crazy. We cannot turn our back from the world from which we earn our living today and from which our future prosperity depends.

Let me briefly outline just how globalised and open we are, after more than two decades of deliberate effort.

In 1999, our exports to the globe account for 114 per cent of our GDP, our imports for 83 per cent of our GDP. In terms of trade, we were 10.8 times more globally engaged than was the United States. In terms of tourists to population, exactly twice as many tourists visited Malaysia as visited the United States.

Foreign investors play a much, much bigger role in the Malaysian economy than they do in the US economy. Foreign banks in Malaysia held 29 per cent of all banking assets in 1999 and accounted for 31.32 per cent of all bank loans. As a share of total banking, foreign banks play a role three times as large in Malaysia as they do in the United States.

Let me now turn to the flow of foreign labour.

As you know, we are now in the second decade of the Second Great Age of Globalisation. In the First Great Age of Globalisation from the middle of the 19th century through La Belle Epoch to World War I, there was not only the free movement of goods and services and the free flow of capital. There was also the free movement of labour, a point that today's capital-poor and labour-rich countries will increasingly note as the globalisation debate heats up. Does anyone doubt that if the

world's balance of political power were different and today's powers-that-be are India and China rather than
the United States and Western Europe, we will today be
discussing not the freest movement of capital, goods
and services but the unfettered cross-border movements of labour, which no doubt will be seen as by far
the most important welfare and prosperity enhancing
sector of globalisation. The WTO in Geneva would probably be what the ILO is today. No doubt the "WLO", the
World Labour Organisation, appropriately situated in
Hong Kong or Colombo would be working day and
night, figuring how to get the stubborn, recalcitrant
OECD countries to agree to a new round of negotiations.

In Malaysia, foreign workers account for more than
20 per cent of all workers. For the United States to be as
open, there would have to be an immediate inflow in excess of 25 million foreign workers.

Malaysians watch American and foreign television,
read foreign newspapers and magazines, in several lan-
guages. We sometimes see American shows even before
they are released in the United States. I wonder how
many Malaysians do not know where Little Rock, Ar-
kansas is, or the names of at least a dozen American
presidents. I wonder how many Americans know the
name of a single Chinese leader or emperor of the last
2,000 years, never mind the name of any Southeast
Asian. I wonder how many Americans watch foreign
television, read foreign newspapers and magazines,
even those in the English language.

In the past, before fees were hiked, when costs were
much lower and there was no concern for foreign exchange, there were years when more than 60,000 young
Malaysians studied abroad. There were years when
there were more Malaysians studying in foreign institu-

tions of higher learning than in Malaysian institutions of higher learning.

More than 50 per cent of the Congressmen and Senators in the United States today do not have a passport. I honestly do not know of any Malaysian Parliamentarian who has not been overseas.

I choose the United States for comparison because US statistics are so readily available and because the United States is so clearly a committed advocate of globalisation, even though it is a comparatively non-globalised economy and a comparatively non-globalised society.

As a country which has so dramatically marketised over the last two decades, as a country that has so dramatically dismantled state capitalism and moved on to private sector capitalism, as country which has so dramatically globalised, perhaps Malaysia can speak with some experience and some legitimacy on the market system, capitalism and globalisation. As someone who is somewhat guilty of marketising, privatising and globalising the Malaysian economy and our society, perhaps I too can speak with some experience and legitimacy.

The bottom line is this: despite all their obvious flaws, weaknesses and dangers, the market system, capitalism and globalisation have a tremendous potential for good.

But the bottom line is also this: the absolute market system, untempered by responsibility and civilisation, is a grave threat to mankind; absolute capitalism, inconsiderate of humanity and caring, is a monster machine for misery and injustice; absolute globalisation, unguided by rationality and sound judgement is perhaps the greatest danger to the world at the dawn of our new century.

I have spent some time on ends and objectives. Let me now turn to means, measures and action.

It is obvious that to ensure the new globalisation in the new world order that we must have, we must work at the global and international level, at the regional level, and within the boundaries of our own national jurisdiction. We must work on all three fronts.

At the global and international level, we must obviously work to strengthen the solidarity of the South. We must not forget the entire South, even as we must build effective, more compact core-groups and action coalitions, which can concert and mobilise on specific issues and agendas—from indebtedness to commodity prices and terms of trade to the digital divide.

As members of the South, we must also build specific action coalitions with Northern NGOs, governments and interests, when and with whom we share a common cause.

We must exploit the small strategic window of opportunity that exists this year and in 2002, afforded by the 4th WTO Ministerial Meeting, the UN High Level Event on Financing for Development and the Rio Plus Ten Summit on Environment, besides the important annual meetings of the WTO and the IMF/ World Bank.

We must not be mere responders to the agendas and negotiating drafts of others. We must be proactive in forwarding our own agendas and our own proposals, to which others will need to respond.

At the WTO, it is absolutely critical that we hold firmly to the firm position taken in Seattle that the present grave imbalances be rectified and that the implementation issues be resolved. We must not agree to a new Round until these issues are satisfactorily settled and until we can all agree to the agenda for any new Round. We need to ensure adequate negotiating and action capacity in Geneva before we enter the perilous halls of negotiation. We must work together to strengthen not only our heads but also our hearts and our hands.

We must beware of the Trojan Horses lining up outside the WTO building. We must be especially careful of the seemingly innocuous issues—such as transparency in government procurement—which are merely first steps down the slippery slope, which will finally end up in our loss of capacity to pursue our national social and socioeconomic policies.

We must build upon the Havana Programme of Action. We must ask UNCTAD to join the process of moving forward to the fundamentals. There are many who have been convinced by the powers-that-be that the old issues of terms of trade are old hat, passé, relics of the past. They are in fact critical keys to our future. We must all fully examine the costs and the consequences of business cartelisation and the escalation of megabusiness mergers, and a lot more.

At the regional level too, there is little time to be lost.

In Asia, I believe that the idea of Asian regional economic cooperation—which was ridiculed and the unwelcome recipient of political bombardment of megatonnage proportions when I first proposed it more than ten years ago—is progressing apace. It must be given greater depth and greater width.

I strongly believe also that it is high time for Asia to establish the Asian Monetary Fund, whatever we choose to call it. We are privileged to have in our midst today one of the inventors and architects of this historic initiative.

We must work on three fronts to ensure a new globalisation in a New World Order. The third front, for those nations that are still free and not yet colonised, is our own domestic jurisdiction. Let no one hoodwink us into thinking that the nation-state is dead. It is not. It is alive and kicking. I believe that it is also the most crucial action front.

It is probably a universal fact of life that no one can do anything to us worse than what we can do to ourselves. Fortunately, it is also probably as true that no one can do anything for us better than what we can do for ourselves.

We must not let absolute globalisation roll all over us. We must make sure that productive globalisation will work for us and for the bounteous benefit of our people. The most important helping hand that we need is at the end of our own right arm.

10

Globalisation at the Service of Mankind or Mankind at the Service of Globalisation?

"Globalisation must be planned and planned carefully. The planning must involve everyone from every part of the globe. It must be for the good of everyone and it must be proven to be good for everyone. It must be implemented slowly, with the biggest effort directed at the least developed parts of the world."

GLOBALISATION is on everyone's lips nowadays. Until the protests in Seattle it was assumed that globalisation was unstoppable, inevitable and definitely the answer to all the social, economic and political problems of the world.

A speech delivered at the International Consultation on Globalisation in Kuala Lumpur, Malaysia, January 31, 2001

Globalisation is obviously a great idea whose time has come. In a world where jet planes and worldwide telecommunication have reduced it to a global village, it is inevitable that globalisation becomes logical and even unavoidable.

But in the past there were also many great ideas which had been accepted as inevitable, but they have all been proven wrong and had to be jettisoned finally.

Republicanism was considered inevitable because feudalism and kings with divine rights had become too oppressive and had to be got rid off. The return to the public was believed to ensure that the public will not oppress itself. But republics had to have leaders and apparently they can be as oppressive and inconsiderate as were the divine kings.

And so to republicanism was added the idea of absolute equality. Socialism and communism were supposed to do this. The aristocrats were to be liquidated and a workers' government would nationalise everything and distribute all earnings to all the workers equally.

It took more than seventy years and the killing of millions before it was realised that a totally egalitarian society just could not work. The great panacea for the ills of human society was apparently not so great after all. The heaven on earth that was promised by the originators of the ideas turned out to be anything but a heaven.

When it was abandoned capitalism claimed victory. During the challenge posed by socialistic egalitarianism the capitalists had restrained themselves. They showed a friendly face. They accommodated some of the egalitarian ideas, and accepted the need for their activities to be regulated.

The governments curbed the more rapacious of their schemes to reap the maximum profit from commerce and industry, especially the finance industry. Monopolies were made illegal.

But now that capitalism had proven superior to egalitarian socialism and communism new ideas for creating a new heaven on earth poured from the mouth of the victors. This new heaven will be built by doing away with regulations, by an absolutely free market, by breaking down the boundaries of nations and creating a single global entity.

Can we be sure that these new ideas, this globalisation will not go the way of the great ideas of the past? Half a century, or maybe a century, down the road will we be still lauding and practising absolute capitalism in a globalised world? Will capitalism not bring about the same misery that will force people to rebel against it and probably overthrow it as violently as the previous great ideas and their proponents were rejected and violently discarded?

These are the things that we should think of before we espouse globalisation too enthusiastically. Globalisation as presently interpreted is the brainchild of absolute capitalism. Its objective is to enlarge the sphere of capitalist activities to the whole world. The capitalists had always resented their confinement to their own countries. They resented the independence of nations with their own systems and policies which prevent their full economic exploitation by those with the capital and the know-how. If the borders of these independent countries could be brought down and a single policy and system for the whole world adopted then capital could move freely and be fully employed to make even more capital. With huge amounts of capital at their disposal they could develop even bigger ambitions.

And so the world is presented with the great idea of a global nation, of globalisation. But this globalisation is to be confined to the free flow of capital across borders.

Most of the countries of the world are capital poor. For some time now foreign investments in these poor countries had helped them to increase their wealth and economic development. Malaysia is a prime example. Foreign investments in the manufacturing industry had propelled this country from an agricultural country to an industrialised country.

Where before Malaysia only exported rubber and tin and later on palm oil, today 82 per cent of Malaysia's exports which total almost US$100 billion is made up of manufactured goods. The inflow of foreign capital into the country has obviously enriched Malaysia. Encouraged by this, Malaysia invited foreign capital to invest in the stock market. Again Malaysia benefited as the share prices shot up and market capitalisation increased tremendously.

But let us look again at the role of foreign capital in these areas. Although the manufacturing plants are foreign-owned but the capital brought in represents only a fraction of the capital invested. A big portion of the capital is borrowed from local banks. So it is not true that there is such a big inflow of foreign capital. What is true is the inflow of foreign know-how in manufacturing and marketing, something that is more essential than just capital.

Still one should not quibble about this as the foreign direct investments in productive capacities definitely contributed to the growth of the Malaysian economy. The government did not expect any direct revenue from foreign investments. Tax holidays were given freely for extended periods. The main benefit derived by the country was the creation of jobs for the people.

Malaysia's unemployment rate is amongst the lowest in the world.

Foreign investments in the stock market tells a slightly different story. Inflow of foreign capital into the stock market pushed up stock prices making Malaysian companies richer than their profits or assets could justify. On the strength of their high share values the companies and local investors were able to borrow much more and to expand their businesses. The economy prospered. But the overpriced shares expose the country to market manipulations.

The strength and health of the Malaysian economy was such that the exchange rate of the ringgit was steady. Business could be done without much need to hedge. The availability of funds locally and the relatively low interest rates made foreign borrowings quite unnecessary for the local business.

In a way Malaysia had globalised earlier than most countries. So confident was Malaysia that the free movements of capital was good for the country that it allowed the ringgit to be freely traded on the foreign exchange market. The market was free to determine the exchange value of the ringgit. For a long time this confidence was justified as the exchange rate fluctuation of the Malaysian ringgit was minimal.

It must be remembered that the great benefits obtained from Malaysia's own globalisation was during the period when capitalism had a friendly face. As has been pointed out, the end of the Cold War removed the need to show this friendly face. And this unfriendliness is exhibited in the General Agreement on Trade and Tariffs (GATT) rounds which dragged on for years. In the meantime the countries had to depend on bilateral trade agreements.

Bilateral trade agreements take into consideration the various interests and constraints faced by each of the countries concerned. The weak countries did not feel too threatened as they could modify the agreements to suit their needs, even though they were not always able to protect themselves against various tariff and non-tariff barriers. But when the World Trade Organisation (WTO) was set up member countries of the GATT had to negotiate multilateral trade agreements. Now the interest of the individual countries could no longer be considered. Instead, general principles were applied equally to all countries, big and small, rich and poor. Such were the general principles which were forced through the WTO that the poorer countries found themselves having to compete with the rich without any consideration for their handicaps. The principal thrust of the WTO agreements was to remove or reduce import duties and to equalise the rates so as to create what is termed a level playing field.

Poor countries depend on import duties to fill their coffers. Their corporate income tax yield very little revenue for them. Doing away with import duty is likely to hurt their finances. Besides, import duties are useful for protecting local or infant industries. Without them local products would have no chance to compete against imports from the highly efficient high-volume industries of the rich.

Still the poor countries did not object to the WTO and the progressive globalisation which was taking place. Then came the currency crisis in East Asia. The countries attacked were amongst the strongest economies in the developing world. Yet simply by devaluing their currencies they were reduced to begging for help.

Countries like Malaysia which in the past had welcomed the flow of foreign capital but which suffered badly when the Malaysian ringgit was devalued cannot but rethink the benefits of globalisation. We consider the free convertibility of the ringgit and the free market in currencies as part of the globalisation process. We had thought that since our economy was strong the ringgit would not be attacked. But then we were told that diseases affecting the currencies of our neighbours are contagious. Although our ringgit was healthy, the sickness of the Thai baht had sickened the ringgit.

Perhaps there is a basis for this. When neighbouring currencies depreciate, the cost of production is supposed to go down and they would be more competitive as exporters. Malaysia was said to be competing with Thailand and the fall in the Thai baht should make our exports less competitive. Our economy would therefore suffer as a result of the devaluation of the Thai baht. It is however doubtful that we would go into deep recession.

Still in anticipation of the economic downturn in Malaysia the currency traders claimed they must get rid of their ringgit. And when they sold the ringgit, its exchange value naturally fell. It should be mentioned here that the currency traders never really held any ringgit. What they did was to borrow the ringgit and shortsell it. They were never in danger of losing any money. They merely saw an opportunity to make quick profit by shortselling the ringgit. The result was to cause the ringgit to devalue just as they had predicted.

The fall in exchange value rendered the country poor in terms of its capacity to pay for imports. And Malaysia imports a lot of essentials, non-essentials and components for its industries. All these became expensive and affected the profitability of companies and impoverished everyone.

When the currency depreciated in exchange rate terms, foreign portfolio investors found that their shares had also depreciated in foreign currency terms even if the share prices did not fall. But the currency turmoil resulted in share prices falling rapidly. Fearing further losses the foreign short-term investors sold off their shares quickly. The result was an even more rapid and deeper fall in share prices. With this the local businesses went into a tailspin, being unable to meet margin calls and to operate. The percentage of non-performing loans leaped and banks began to show signs of strain.

By now the economy had become really bad and needed to be helped. For the tiger economies of East Asia the only help was from the International Monetary Fund (IMF). But the Fund was not going to help without extracting some concession. Accusing the countries of irresponsible governance, of corruption and cronyism, the IMF demanded that loans would only be given if the countries submitted to IMF control over the economy and open up their countries to foreign business. What this means is that foreign banks and businesses could operate completely without restriction in the countries getting IMF loans. Additionally the foreign banks and investors should be free to pick up the shares of the local banks and business at the low prices which the dumping of their shares by foreign investors had caused.

It seems to many that it was grossly unfair for the people who had pushed down the share prices to be allowed to buy the shares at the depreciated prices. They may not have deliberately devalued the shares but whether deliberate or not it was they who caused the stock market to plunge. Now they are benefiting from this plunge.

But then we are told that that is how the free market operates. Indeed the free market is disciplining the governments and forcing them to give up their corruption, cronyism, etc. It seems that it is necessary to destroy their economies along with a lot of innocent people in order to punish them.

Unfortunately, for many rebuilding has not been as easy as destroying. Many of the economies destroyed by this particular manifestation of globalisation have yet to recover.

In the face of this can we just continue accepting globalisation unquestioningly? What we foresee is more assaults on the economies of the weak countries by the strong in the future. Or we may lose control of our economies to the foreign banks and businesses.

We see, for example, the formation of giant banks and corporations belonging to the rich countries. Each one of these entities is now much bigger than any one of the developing countries. Once the borders are down these giants will move in to compete with the puny banks and corporations of the developing countries. The field may be level but the contest will not be between equals. There is no doubt that the giants are going to win. In the end the banks and businesses of the developing countries will be bankrupted and will be gobbled up by the foreign giants.

Perhaps this will improve efficiency. Perhaps the locals working for the foreign giants will get better pay and perks. But will foreign ownership of all the wealth of these countries be in the interest of the countries and people?

Most of the developing countries have programmes for wealth distribution in order to solve social problems. In Malaysia we have to help the deprived indigenous community get a fair share of the wealth of the country through an affirmative action programme. This programme undoubtedly affects the productivity and effi-

107

ciency of businesses. But it is good for avoiding racial tension and disruptive activities which can damage business even more.

Foreign owners are not interested in the social problems of countries. They want to maximise profits. The governments will have to tackle social and political problems. So when the economy is totally in foreign hands it is likely that social unrest will increase.

But then those who control the economy would also like to ensure that the governments are business-friendly. If the governments are not cooperative enough then the governments should be changed. This involves interference in internal politics. But powerful foreign business would not be too particular about not interfering in local affairs. In subtle ways or overtly they will interfere. The result is a loss of independence for the country.

Maybe we are imagining these things. Maybe globalisation will not result in the loss of a country's independence. But can we be sure? There really is no assurance this would not happen.

We have seen how much the IMF interferes in the internal affairs of the countries which borrowed its money. Leaders and governments had to be changed according to the wishes of the IMF and other international agencies.

Malaysia is a recalcitrant. Malaysia is a heretic. Malaysia is cynical about globalisation. But it is not globalisation per se. It is the current interpretation of globalisation. Globalisation and the free market should not mean capital flows only. Even if it does, it should accept some form of regulation so that economic turmoils will not be the result. It has been pointed out that free trade under the WTO is not free, it is regulated. So why shouldn't the process of globalisation be regulated?

The WTO must allow a degree of regulation to be instituted by member countries when the competition is not between equals. Certain practices must be allowed. There is no necessity to have only a few big companies. Let there be many companies, big and small. Let them compete with handicaps. If you can accept that in golf, why not in trade?

Give time for adjustments, for equalising the forces. In Japan, some ten corporations produce electronic products. They compete in the same markets. They continuously improve and innovate. They seem to see no necessity to acquire each other or to merge or to swallow small players in order to become efficient. We don't see any harm in their remaining separate. We still enjoy their low-priced high quality products.

Then there are the workers. For countries like India and China their people are their capital. Already the brainy amongst them are being enticed away. Why not also allow a free flow of human capital. Countries with excess workers should be permitted to export them to countries short of workers and plagued with high cost labour. The productivity of the world will certainly improve. And this should be good for globalisation.

Then there is the need for time to effect the changes required by globalisation. Change destabilises and rapid change destabilises most of all. We should allow ourselves more time to change into a globalised economy. Those who are ready, those who are rich should change first. The others can follow according to their capacities, pausing to make corrections, learning from those who had changed earlier, adjusting and consolidating.

The world of today is very rich because of a combination of natural resources and the technologies that Man has developed. There is really no reason why, in a caring world, anyone should be poor. Africa, Central Asia, South America and the South Pacific can easily be enriched by investing the huge surplus of capital in developmental and productive capacities. If the world is to be a global entity then there should not be abject poverty in some parts and obscene wealth in other parts. All must be reasonably well off. Capital combined with modern technology have the capacity to enrich the whole globe. We can invest in a powerful railway system to carry the raw materials and imports of Central Asia at low cost. We can develop the great rivers of Latin America, Africa and Asia into the kind of transportation channels that the Rhine and the Danube are to Europe. We can transport excess fresh water from melting snow to the arid deserts of the world much in the same way that oil and gas are now being piped over thousands of miles. We can do a whole lot of things that can lend true meaning to globalisation.

Surely globalisation must involve the whole world. Today when we talk about globalisation we think only of those countries with developed or developing markets. We think of opening up existing markets. We think of maximising our profits. But we are really not thinking about the world, about the globe which encompasses the familiar and the unfamiliar and inaccessible areas. Yet what is more reasonable and logical than to think of globalisation which involves the whole world. It is not too far-fetched an idea. We only have to change our mindsets. And if we accept globalisation to mean the development of the whole world by the international community, slowly at first but more rapidly later we can really become a global community, a globalised world.

No one has a monopoly on ideas. I know, of course, that what I say here will never be reported by the world press. Nobody outside this hall will hear of it. But even if you as participants will not want to consider a globalisation which is more literal, a globalisation that involves the whole globe; even if you will not discuss this preposterous idea, I am happy because I have this opportunity to propound my ideas on the real globalisation. A globalisation which involves only a fraction of the world is not globalisation. A globalisation that involves only capital flows and predatory assaults on the weak by the strong is not globalisation. A globalisation that benefits the few and destroys the many is not globalisation. And a hurried grab at the spoils is not globalisation.

Globalisation must be planned and planned carefully. The planning must involve everyone from every part of the globe. It must be for the good of everyone and it must be proven to be good for everyone. It must be implemented slowly, with the biggest effort directed at the least developed parts of the world.

Market principles must be retained. The making of profit should not be regarded as a sin, but profiteering, the exploitation of the poor and the gullible by the rich and the smart, should be made punishable by the international community.

There should be free movement of capital and labour but not to the detriment of the countries involved. The world's productivity must be increased and disparities of all kinds minimised.

I don't think we can do all these in our lifetime or even in two lifetimes. But we should begin. And we should begin by thinking about it, thinking about globalisation as a sharing of the wealth of the world in raw material, capital, labour and technology, a sharing that is not equal but fair.

This is globalisation in the service of mankind. Globalisation must serve us and not the other way round.

11

Malaysia's Approach to Globalisation

"Malaysia has experienced the globalisation of capital and we were nearly destroyed by it. Fortunately, we were able to develop our own methods to defend ourselves and rebuild our economy. We know that our success may be shortlived but we are not going to allow ourselves to be sold ideas, ideologies and slogans without carefully examining them. If we find the slightest suspicion that another agenda is being promoted we will fight tooth and nail to defend our country and the prosperity of our people."

MALAYSIA'S approach to globalisation in general and the financial crisis in particular has been guided by the basic principle that the pace of globalisation in Malaysia at least must be on Malaysia's terms, based on its circumstances and priorities. It may not always be possible but it is crucial to ensure that

A speech delivered at Cairo University in Cairo, Egypt, on June 20, 2000 everybody benefits—both the foreign investors and Malaysians. A step-by-step approach is also important to avoid the excesses and problems associated with all new ideas, principles or processes, including globalisation. We need as always to be pragmatic and flexible, not dogmatic in pursuing globalisation. It cannot be viewed as an end in itself, but as a means to an end, which is a better life for our people and our continued freedom from foreign domination.

Just as absolute freedom leads to anarchy, so too, "absolute globalisation" could lead to chaos, as demonstrated by the Asian financial crisis. We must avoid the tyranny of "free markets", where power comes not from the barrel of a gun, but from the checkbook. We do not subscribe to the view that market discipline is infallible, because markets have never been perfect and have a strong tendency to overreact and to be subjected to manipulations.

The industrial countries took more than a hundred years to reach the present stage of their development before they propose to adopt globalisation and liberalisation. It is unfair to expect developing countries to liberalise and do away with the protection of their borders at the same instant the developed countries do.

The Asian financial crisis has brought to the forefront the risks and challenges that globalisation poses to developing countries, particularly small open economies such as Malaysia. Initial denial has now been replaced by a reluctant acceptance of the need to address the problems of destabilising capital flows often associated with the activities of currency speculators, hedge funds and short-term investors. The crisis has also heightened the call for reforms in the international financial architecture. The so-called caretaker of the international financial system, the International Monetary Fund (IMF) has been widely criticised for its mismanagement of the crisis. Questions have also been raised about the role of the World Trade Organisation (WTO) in contributing to global instability by "encouraging" developing countries to liberalise too rapidly. After more than two years of painful policy adjustments and social upheavals, erosion of incomes and loss of dignity or "face", the crisis-affected Asian economies of Indonesia, Thailand, South Korea and Malaysia have turned around, a few with growth rates now exceeding pre-crisis levels. Despite the initial scepticism, Malaysia's rejection of the IMF formula and loans and its decision to regain exchange rate control and regulate the flows of short-term capital have now been accepted, though reluctantly, as a viable alternative in crisis management.

The initial international reaction when on September 1, 1998 we introduced selective capital and exchange control was to condemn Malaysia. It was said:

(a) that Malaysia was turning its back on the free-market system;

(b) that capital controls were regressive and will lead to all sorts of inefficiencies;

(c) that the controls were a case of closing the barn door after the horse has bolted;

(d) that Malaysia's resort to controls was to avoid economic and financial restructuring;

(e) that the Malaysian government feared being overthrown like the Indonesian government; and

(f) that Malaysia was inherently against the IMF for no very good reason.

The truth of the matter is that at the beginning of the crisis, we did adopt policies similar to the IMF approach. We were told that the IMF policies of tight fiscal and monetary policies would restore market confidence and stability. Unfortunately, these policies not only did not restore confidence, but actually aggravated the crisis, as the reduction in government expenditure reinforced the contraction in domestic demand, while higher interest rates and a credit squeeze took their toll on the balance sheets of the corporate and banking sectors. When we saw that tight fiscal and monetary policy was deepening the recession in the IMF-programme countries and in Malaysia as well, we decided to look for alternative solutions to restore stability and ensure economic recovery.

The reasons why the IMF policy recipe failed in Asia are now well known. The basic problem, of course, was that the IMF misdiagnosed the problems in Asia and applied the same remedies that were used in Latin America before. Because of its background and expertise, the IMF tends to look at macroeconomic variables, and missed out the crucial details in the crisis countries. This led to policies that were not suitable for the problem at hand. From the beginning, the IMF viewed the crisis as a small and temporary problem. It did not believe the information on the ground of the size of the hedge funds, their staying power and their unlimited greed. Consequently, the IMF underestimated the duration and depth of the currency depreciation.

The crisis also worsened because the IMF is principally concerned with repayment of debts imprudently made by commercial banks to the countries concerned. The IMF programmes also did not take into consideration the specific conditions in individual crisis countries, such as the degree of foreign borrowings of both the governments and the private sectors. Consequently, the IMF's recommendations of higher interest rates simply weakened the capacity to repay loans by and the viability of the indebted businesses and the government. The IMF also underestimated the impact of its recommendations on the financial system. Forced closure of banks led to a loss of confidence in surviving banks and the breakdown of the intermediation system. Similarly, policies that arbitrarily removed monopolies and subsidies in the existing economic system led to higher costs and the breakdown of the distribution system. As a result, inflation soared to levels beyond what was warranted by the currency depreciation. Another error in judgement by the IMF was the lack of understanding of the close links between the foreign exchange market and stock market, which can reinforce each other in depreciating the exchange rate and depressing the value of stock prices. The decline in stock prices made debtors of previously healthy companies and investors. Non-performing loans increased and the surviving banks began to fail. Market capitalisation shrank to a fraction of its original value resulting in real loss as margin calls on loans could not be met, further increasing the percentage of NPLs. The IMF also shortened the period for declaring loans as non-performing from six months to three months. The effect on business and banks was disastrous.

It should be remembered that fixed exchange rates were not incompatible with the free market. The Bretton Woods agreements to revive world trade was actually based on the fixed exchange rate. In deciding to fix the exchange rate of the Malaysian ringgit with the US dollar, Malaysia was therefore not renouncing the free market. We have always subscribed to and will continue to believe in the free market. We cannot do otherwise as we are a trading nation, in fact the 17th biggest trading nation in the world. Far from being incompatible with

117

the free market, the fixed exchange rate actually facilitated trade and contributed towards recovery and rapid growth. The only thing that the exchange rate control did was to keep the currency out of the hands of speculators, who are after all not necessary for trade or the economy. With the fixed exchanged rate it was possible to take various measures to revive the economy without fear of the speculators deliberately devaluing the currency.

Some commentators have suggested that Malaysia need not have imposed the exchange controls. They pointed out that the regional currencies were all beginning to recover in the last quarter of 1998, suggesting that Malaysia had shut the door after the horse had bolted. It is easy to say that now, but at that point in time, everyone, including the great economic experts, were predicting continued depression of the Asian economy. They said that we had not struck bottom yet. What could have caused the Asian economy to recover was the fear on the part of currency traders that many Asian countries would have adopted Malaysia's exchange rate control. This would have resulted in huge losses for the currency speculators. And so they reduced their speculations. But a contributory cause to their reduced activities could be that at about this time the LTCM Fund lost its bet on the Russian ruble and threatened to destabilise the US financial institutions completely. Suddenly, currency speculation became a dangerous game for the rich countries and it was stopped.

In Malaysia's case, instability in the ringgit exchange rate was aggravated by outflows of the ringgit to offshore markets. The situation in Malaysia was peculiar in that we had a very liberal foreign exchange regime, which led to the buildup of a large offshore ringgit market. While Malaysia had curtailed ringgit borrowings to finance currency trading, ringgit funds were available from banks in Singapore, which offered rates as high as 20 to 30 per cent. Although the cost of borrowing foreign ringgit was high, the need to borrow for shortselling was only for a brief period and the profits were very high. Malaysia could not compete by raising interest rates because this would adversely affect business in Malaysia. To prevent this haemorrhage we stopped the movement of the ringgit across our border. If the ringgit held outside the country was not returned within a month then they will not be allowed to return at all. Effectively this meant they will have no value at all after a month. Foreign holders of the currency had to return it to Malaysia. This measure stopped the flow of the ringgit to Singapore and deprived the currency traders from access to the ringgit to speculate with. With the banks flushed with repatriated money it was possible to lower interest rates, thus reducing the cost of doing business. Fortunately, Malaysia achieved a huge trade surplus during the turmoil, earning Malaysia sufficient foreign exchange to pay for imports.

Control over short-term capital was in the form of a moratorium on expatriation of short-term investment funds for a period of one year. Profits could be taken out of the country and so could the receipts from the sale of assets of foreign direct investments. As a result of this control on short-term speculative money, the share market recovered rapidly. By the end of the moratorium period, the market had gained by about 200 per cent and when the moratorium was lifted one year after the predicted massive outflow of capital did not take place. The stock market index remained high.

Malaysia was very conscious that its decision to control the exchange rate was a move fraught with danger. In the first place it was going against accepted current wisdom and it would be faced with a very hostile reaction by the international financial community, including the IMF, the World Bank and the most powerful country in the world. Clearly, it was going to frustrate the rich investors who had invested huge sums of money in the hedge funds and were getting as much as 30 per cent return on them. If they could they would try to ensure that Malaysian control failed. When Malaysia tried to borrow from abroad to finance local projects the rates shot up so that the loan had to be aborted. Other actions were also taken to prevent Malaysia's economic recovery, including reporting that Malaysia is dangerous for tourism.

Malaysia knew there were dangers but to submit would bring about a fate that would be worse. We would lose our independence and our honour. On the other hand, if we succeeded we would remain independent, even if our economy might not do so well.

Still we needed to ensure that there would be a reasonable chance of success. Despite charges that Malaysia had been profligate and had expanded too much on the so-called megaprojects, financially Malaysia was and is very sound. Neither the government nor the private sector had borrowed much from foreign sources. The need for foreign exchange to repay loans was insignificant. But the greatest strength lies in Malaysia's high savings rate of almost 40 per cent of GDP. We had sufficient internal financial resources to support our recovery. Even when the foreign rating agencies downgraded us, it did not hurt. We have huge amounts of ringgit and our foreign reserves could at that time finance more than three months of retained imports. (Today, it is six months.) We were therefore quite confident that if our controls fail we would not be forced to beg, at least not for a long time.

As it turned out the signs of recovery appeared almost immediately after the controls were instituted. The banking system was flushed with money, which had been brought back, and low interest rates revived ailing businesses. The stock market recovered. Trade surpluses increased and contributed towards higher reserves. The fixed exchange rate made hedging unnecessary, reducing the cost of doing business and increasing profits.

The GDP, which had contracted by 7 per cent in 1998, achieved a 5.6 per cent growth in 1999. Domestic consumption shot up, creating a sense of well-being for all. Inflation was within manageable levels.

Malaysia had no unemployment problem and had always had to import labour. The downturn affected foreign labour largely. The few Malaysians who had been laid off found new jobs. With recovery wages improved.

Still as a result of the economic recession many companies and individuals had to face financial difficulties. The non-performing loans which before the turmoil was only 3 per cent rose to 17 per cent plus. The government set up an asset management company, which purchased all the big NPLs at a discount. This enabled the distressed companies to borrow again and the banks to be back in business. Other less affected companies had their loans restructured with the help of the Corporate Debt Restructuring Committee (CDRC). The banks were refinanced through a capital fund established by the government.

All these funds helped distressed companies to recover, to regain profitability and to contribute to the government coffers through corporate taxes.

The IMF's principal objective was to prise open the beleaguered country's market so that foreign companies could move in to take over local businesses. The raids by foreign predators are made less costly because the pullout of short-term capital from the stock market lowered share prices to rock-bottom levels. Some countries resisted but others have now lost all their good companies and banks, including the newly privatised utility companies. Privatisation was encouraged by the IMF because locals were unable to participate and foreigners could pick the choicest items.

Since Malaysia is not under the IMF we are able to keep off the foreign predators. But now the attack is coming from another direction. Globalisation and information technology are making local companies uncompetitive and their failure will result in foreign takeovers. We are trying to find out how to counter these new assaults.

The propaganda machine of the West is good at making everyone feel guilty if he does not accept the new ideas and ideologies created by the rich to give them ever more advantage over the poor. Democracy, the free market, a world without borders, liberalism, labour rights and child labour, etc, have all been cooked up in the rich countries and then forced on the poor. They all sound great but somehow their acceptance by the poor invariably destabilise them and put them at the mercy of the rich.

The free market is a case in point. Malaysia subscribes to the free market but now we are told that governments are superfluous, as the free market will determine the level and the manner of economic growth. It seems that the free market will actually discipline governments, making them more accountable, transparent and less corrupt. But markets exist in order to enable investors to make money and maximise profits; not to cater to a nation's need or society's welfare. Businessmen are not elected by the people to look after their welfare.

If they are elected at all, it is by the shareholders. And shareholders are interested in returns and capital gains for themselves only. It is therefore ridiculous to think that the free market will discipline governments for the good of nations or society. Governments, especially democratic governments, owe it to their constituents to ensure the wellbeing and development of the nations.

Yet today people talk of the free market as if it is a religion that everyone must accept. To question its role in shaping the economic development of the world is to commit heresy. The free market must be embraced and upheld by everyone, rich and poor.

However, the free market is no more than a new name for capitalism, unbridled capitalism. The size of the capital involved today is unbelievable. It is said that the trade in currency, which is what capital is all about, is twenty times bigger than world trade. Such a huge sum of money cannot but disrupt businesses wherever it goes. When used to buy and sell currencies economies can be totally disrupted, enriching the money movers and impoverishing whole nations, exploding into riots, violence and wars, overthrowing governments and spreading anarchy where law and order had prevailed. Still the free market or unbridled capitalism is defended.

It is time that we, the poor in particular, recognise that we are being led up the garden path by the sweet words and promises of the new slogans, new systems and new ideologies. We recognise that we cannot go backwards. We cannot go back to the centrally planned economy of the socialist and communist. But is it necessary that the way forward should be the one shown to us by the rich and the powerful? Cannot the market be free without its domination by the rich and the powerful? Indeed, is a free market free if it is dominated by the rich?

Malaysia has experienced the globalisation of capital and we were nearly destroyed by it. Fortunately, we were able to develop our own methods to defend ourselves and rebuild our economy. We know that our success may be shortlived but we are not going to allow ourselves to be sold ideas, ideologies and slogans without carefully examining them. If we find the slightest suspicion that another agenda is being promoted we will fight tooth and nail to defend our country and the prosperity of our people.

12

Making Globalisation Work

"A globalised world would be meaningless unless it is an enriched and an equitable world. Deregulation, borderlessness, free flow of capital while enriching the already rich must also contribute towards the rapid and equitable growth of the poor. They should also enrich the world."

THE past three decades have seen a rapid pace of integration of the global economy. Anything that happens in a country's economy must have some effect on the economy of the world. Thus the collapse of the economy in a small country may cut off the world's supply of some products which would then affect the pricing of goods involving that product. The col-

A speech delivered at the Commonwealth Business Forum in Johannesburg, South Africa, on November 10, 1999

lapse may be due to natural causes or political upheavals but the effect is the same. In the most extreme case the gyrations of the New York Stock Exchange (NYSE) will be followed by similar gyrations in the stock exchanges of the world although the businesses and companies and the banks of the different countries have nothing to do with the NYSE.

No country can isolate or insulate its economy from the rest of the world. In one way or another the performance of the economy would depend on the economic situation in the rest of the world. This inability to insulate is made worse by the speed of communication. Every little thing that happens anywhere is communicated to the rest of the world in real time. And invariably they have an economic dimension. Thus, if there is a drought in Brazil, coffee prices would go up. If there is a demonstration in a country, tourists would cancel their visits and investors would put their money in another country.

All these would, of course, have an effect on the economies of nations, bad for some and good for others. Speculators love this. They would have a field day shuffling their capital from one country to another in pursuit of profit maximisation.

But what if the reports through the wire services are false or fabricated? What if the speculators invent rumours or make wrong forecasts deliberately or otherwise? The countries targeted would lose money as speculators dump their holdings of shares or commodities. People would suffer as they lose their means of livelihood. There may be riots and even bloodshed. All because some speculators want to make money for themselves.

How does a businessman (or a country for that matter) insure himself against the gyrations of supplies and prices. Hedging is the answer. By buying or selling forward or by purchasing hard currencies, the effect of the uncertainties, whether real or manipulated, can be minimised. Indeed, the smart ones can actually make money purely through hedging.

And so a new business is born. This is the business of insuring against gyrations in prices and in exchange rate fluctuations. It started off innocently enough as insurance against the unpredictable and the unexpected. It is a kind of gambling. Sometimes the hedger makes, sometimes the hedge funds make. It was all still fair and square.

But then the hedge funds found that they can easily manipulate the unknown and the unpredictable so as to win and profit every time all the time. The theory is as old as commerce itself. If you are big enough to monopolise then you can make certain of the prices by being able to fix them. Since you own all the supplies you are in a position to demand to be paid the price you name.

But why own the commodity? Why not simply control the supply of the commodity? This can be done simply by putting a small deposit on future supplies. If the supplies are not taken up only the deposit would be forfeited. On the other hand, if the prices go up huge profits can be made.

Forward selling of non-existent commodities can also be made if there is a possibility that the price would fall below the price sold. That way the commodity could be bought at the lower price and delivered to the buyer who had bought at the higher price. Eventually real goods or commodities need not be involved at all. Fictitious goods were sold at current price for delivery later when the real goods have gone down in price and could be bought for delivery.

If commodities and goods can be traded in this virtual way, why not money itself? And so money or currency became commodities to be traded in the same way.

The price of everything is determined by the willingness of a buyer to buy. To sell the price must be lowered until a willing buyer is found. The result is rapid fall in prices as more and more of the virtual commodity is offered.

In a borderless world the players with unlimited money can offer any amount of any commodity worldwide at continuously lower prices. The actual producers of the commodity will find the prices falling below cost resulting in huge losses. The real traders in real goods will often lose money but the speculators and manipulators will make huge sums without ever owning or taking delivery of any real goods, commodities or currencies. And whole countries and their governments can go bankrupt because their products fetch prices below costs and their currencies lose their value. The loss is not just economic or financial but also social and political. Governments can and have actually fallen because of this trade in non-existent commodities, including money. Thus when globalisation enables free flow of capital, serious abuses can take place.

Yet globalisation can bring about a lot of good to the poor countries. If the poor try to raise themselves up by their bootstraps the process and the pace would be so slow that it would only result in their being left further and further behind. For the poor countries it would be like having to invent the wheel. But if the rich with their money, technology and marketing know-how were to invest in the poor countries not only will the poor see big inflows of capital but they would acquire the skills and the technology to make quantum leaps in order to catch up with the rich. Thus with the technology and capital, rich countries through their multinationals can set up production facilities in the poor countries in order to take advantage of lower labour and other costs. The workers in the poor countries gain employment, incomes and skills. Their country gains through reduction in unemployment and through the injection of funds into its systems. Eventually these countries would learn enough about management and technology to start their own industries bringing even greater benefit to their people. And in time a poor technologically deprived country can become industrialised through this process. In the case of Malaysia, from being a country dependent on the production and export of only two commodities, tin and rubber, it has now become a significant exporter of manufactured goods. Today 80 per cent of Malaysian export is made up of manufactured goods. The per capita income of the country rose from US$300 to almost US$5,000 before the economic turmoil of 1997-1998. Thus the opening up of its borders to foreign capital and know-how has benefited Malaysia tremendously. And it should benefit other developing countries as much if conditions are made suitable for the inflow of direct foreign investments.

Clearly, globalisation and the borderless world have their up side and down side. They are not a panacea for all economic ills. While they can enrich the poor, they can also impoverish and even destroy the economies of countries and regions.

Globalisation is a concept invented by Man and as such it is not perfect. It can bring about a lot of good but it can also lend itself to abuses and give forth some of the most tragic results. Globalisation cannot be embraced in toto simply because it enables the free movement of capital and trade. Free movement by itself does not bring benefit. For whereas capital inflow can create wealth, capital outflow, particularly rapid capital out-flow, can bring about economic and financial disaster.

As with every system invented by Man, good can only come about if the system is properly understood and managed. This is because there are always rogue elements in human societies and they will always abuse the system in order to reap high returns, whether economic, social or political. To minimise abuses all systems must be regulated.

Unfortunately, in their enthusiasm, the great trading nations have insisted that along with globalisation there must also be total deregulation. They believe the market will correct itself. This is called the discipline of the market. In fact, they believe the market will actually discipline the governments, forcing them to be less corrupt and more transparent.

Idealists are always blind to the contrariness of human nature. Market players are not the most caring people. Their obsession is with profits at whatever cost to others. They are not particularly concerned about society and its well-being. The idea that governments, especially elected governments, should surrender societal care to the market is as welcome as letting wolves to guard sheep.

The world is nevertheless going through a process of dismantling rules, regulations and laws governing capital flows and trade in goods and services. The World Trade Organisation (WTO) is forcing the pace simply because globalisation and deregulation are considered to be good in themselves and not because of the results they produce. And so when recently the free capital flows destroyed the economies of whole regions, the free-market idealists refuse to recognise anything wrong with the system. They blame the lack of transparency and corruption of the governments instead. That these same governments had obviously succeeded in rapidly developing their countries until the free market-eers attacked them is ignored. The free market just cannot be wrong. Only non-believers and heretics will fail to acknowledge this. As we all know the only way to deal with heretics is to burn them at the stakes. And figuratively that is what was done to the free-market non-believers.

A level playing field is a term invented by the rich to imply fair competition. But merely because the field is level is not enough for fairness and equitability to be achieved. The players on the field must also be evenly matched. In sports handicaps are common simply because it is acknowledged that certain participants are disadvantaged. In fact, it is common in sports to grade teams according to their ages and sizes. A heavyweight boxer will never be pitted against a featherweight no matter how well constructed and level the ring is.

Yet the emphasis in trade and investments is solely on level playing fields. If globalisation is going to benefit the world, then the relative strengths of the trading partners must also be given due consideration. It will not cost the superior partners much if handicaps are given to the weaker partners. Indeed in the long run it will benefit the superior partner also, for the prosperity achieved by the weaker partner due to the privileges will make it a much more viable market, a market that is sustainable for the rich.

Just as we should rethink globalisation and deregulation, we should talk no more of level playing fields without talking also about the relative strengths of the parties concerned and the need to award handicaps. One should remember that it took the developed countries of Europe almost 50 years to bring down their trade barriers against each other and even then not completely. And the European countries are more evenly developed than the other countries of the world today. Surely a globalised world should not be equated with the union of the European countries where borders are now more or less removed, and access is more or less open to everyone. Probably over a period of centuries the countries of the world can be expected to do away with borders and become as unified as Europe. But many people have only just emerged from colonial bondage and they value the little freedom that they have too much to become apparently equal citizens of the globe. They suspect that they would not be really equal citizens. They suspect that they would once again revert to being subjects of the strong and the powerful, who only incidentally happen to be their former colonial masters.

Provided handicaps and privileges are accorded the weak countries, provided that certain rules and regulations remain, there is every possibility that globalisation will help the developing countries to catch up with the developed. In fact, in certain areas they can be actually strong and competitive. Thus where natural products and labour are of prime importance they can be actually more competitive than the developed countries whose commodities have been used up and whose labour cost is extremely high.

There is a need also to consider the terms of trade. For decades now the commodities produced by the poor countries have appreciated in price at a slower rate than the manufactured products they import from the rich. This means that the poor have to sell more and more of their commodities in order to buy less and less of the imported goods they need. The result is that the poor are getting poorer while the rich are getting richer.

The rules of supply and demand, of market forces, must of course prevail. But the prices of commodities are not always governed by these rules. Far too frequently the prices are determined by speculators, their forward purchases and their shortselling activities. Invariably the poor producing countries are the losers for they are not involved in speculative trading.

On the other hand, the cost of the goods they buy are often the result of artificially inflated costs, including the very high wages paid and the high cost of other services in developed countries. Since the cost of raw materials is usually a small fraction of total cost, can't the rich simply pay more for their raw material imports? Market forces may not be involved when doing this but must market forces always take precedence over human welfare?

If trade is to be equitable, then the problem of the terms of trade must be addressed. The poor commodity producers must be paid higher prices roughly in keeping with the rise in the price of the manufactured goods which they import. In the long run the rich would still benefit for when the poor commodity producers are enriched through better prices, they will make better markets for the products of the rich.

A globalised world would be meaningless unless it is an enriched and equitable world. Deregulation, borderlessness, free flow of capital while enriching the already rich must also contribute towards the rapid and equitable growth of the poor. They should also enrich the world. It is not globalisation or deregulation or borderlessness or free capital flows which is important. It is what they can do for world trade, for economic growth and for alleviating the poverty of the world that is important. If they can, then we should all welcome these ideas and concepts. If they don't, if they bring about more misery to the already miserable, then, notwithstanding their being in keeping with the times, notwithstanding the advances in technology, the rapidity of communication, etc, they should all be rejected.

The purpose of commerce is not merely to make money for some people. Commerce is undertaken because of the need to meet demands for goods and services. Meeting these demands is the *raison d'etre* of trade and profit is actually a by-product of meeting these needs.

The great marketeers of the world have since made trade as a milch cow, solely as a generator of profits. With this, real demand has been made subordinate to the making of money by creating demand where there is no demand. Thus exchange rates of currencies are needed in order to facilitate trade. The amount required is only to cover the actual cost of the goods traded. But the currency traders created a market in currency, created demands which have no relation whatsoever to the actual trading needs. In the end trade in currency has become 20 times bigger than world trade and huge profits are made through a totally artificial demand and supply. There is not that much of money in the world, but no matter. Even if the currency does not exist, trade in it can still take place, and huge profits can still be made. The misery that these profiteers create is a matter of no consequence, for trade is no longer about meeting the demands for goods and services. Trade is just about trade, the serious business of making money in any way at any cost.

Globalisation, as presently interpreted, simply means the enlarging of the area and the potential for those with the means to make even more money for themselves. What happens to those without the means does not seem to matter. In fact, what happens to anybody else, to society at large, to nations and regions does not matter. Only the profits for the traders matter. And so free flows of capital have decimated the wealth of the tiger economies of East Asia. Sadly, the currency traders gain only a fraction of the wealth they destroyed as their profit. Obviously for the world there is a net loss of wealth.

If globalisation is good for the world then everyone should benefit from it. Obviously it is not only not benefiting everyone but it is hurting many. We need to rethink globalisation and reinterpret it.

The Commonwealth is a grouping of rich and poor nations bound by historical ties, an ability to speak a common language and a roughly common system of government and laws. Without doubt our worldview, our perception of things are also roughly similar. We still have the capacity to think our own thoughts and to act on them together. With the considerable influence we wield we have often been a force for the good. With regard to globalisation we need to ensure that our members and other countries do not suffer because our individual voices are insignificant in the WTO especially. We need to achieve a consensus on globalisation and then we should speak with one voice, especially in the WTO.

Globalisation may be an idea whose time has come but that alone should not mean we should all meekly accept it. We must ensure that it will be for our good, individually and collectively, before we do. Some of us have already had considerable experience of the globalised free flows of capital. We have benefited but we have also suffered when there are abuses. Our experiences must be used to devise and improve the idea of globalisation so as to reduce the abuses and so help realise the good that globalisation promises.

The Commonwealth is a representative segment of the world. Perhaps we should try our interpretation of globalisation amongst us first. We should devise rules and regulations for capital flows so that there will be economic stability rather than turmoil. Free trade need not be full of uncertainties and tumult. There need not be excessive gambling and speculation simply because free trade enables them. If in order to benefit all some regulations have to be put in place, there is no reason why not. Trade has benefited the world immensely. Currency trading is said to be 20 times bigger than world trade. But what do we have to show for it? The world is not 20 times richer. Instead the world is very much poorer. True, a few currency traders and banks have become extremely rich. But surely trade is not about making a few people very, very rich. As I said earlier, trade is about supplying needs and demands. This is basic and when we find trade has been abused, bringing disaster with it, we have to go back to basics.

If the Commonwealth wants to see trade and investment flows bringing with them prosperity in a globalised world, the Commonwealth must be willing to challenge conventional wisdom and propose rules and regulations to make free trade create wealth and not destroy it.

13

Globalisation and Smart Partnership

"Globalisation, a borderless world, is already a fact. In the field of information distribution and e-commerce, borders mean very little now. But the fact that globalisation has come (and is apparently irresistible) does not mean we should just sit by and watch as the predators destroy us."

THERE is no doubt that globalisation is an idea whose time has come. All of us must therefore be prepared to accept it. But whereas the idea has come, it is far from clear. So far the interpretation or definition of globalisation has been made largely by the rich countries. Not surprisingly the interpretation of the concept would result in gains by them. If they are the only ones to gain, whether the idea is timely or not,

A speech delivered at the 4th Langkawi International Dialogue in Langkawi, Malaysia, on July 25, 1999

there is no very good reason why the poor countries must also accept globalisation.

There was a time when the idea of colonisation and imperialism was acceptable. It was natural almost for European nations to colonise the rest of the world. Even the smallest European nations regarded it *de rigueur* for them to acquire vast territories in Africa, Asia and South America and rule them as colonies.

For a long time, no one, not even the colonised Asians or Africans, questioned the rights of the European to occupy and rule their lands. Europeans even invented the idea of their God-given right and responsibility to rule. It was the White Man's burden. They have been especially chosen to bring their civilising influences to the natives, sometimes referred to as the savages.

When an idea has come and is accepted it becomes so entrenched that it is very difficult to say or do anything that is against it. To do so would involve charges of heresy. The dissenter becomes the object of universal opprobrium. He is castigated by all and shunned even by his friends or his own kind.

It takes time for the defects and ill-effects of the idea to emerge and to be recognised. Thus communism and socialism as ideologies may not be criticised or rejected where these ideologies had become accepted. Everyone, whether he believed in them or not, would sing their praises. Not to do so would incur the wrath of the community or people. Of course, it may result in painful punishment, even death in many cases.

The fact that when these ideologies were introduced one of the objectives was to banish the oppression of feudalism or capitalism did not prevent the communists and socialists from indulging in the same kind of oppression when they were in power. It would seem that oppression is only bad if it is imposed by others against oneself. If one gets into power and indulges in the same kind of oppression against others, it is acceptable.

Thus the rule of the Czar of Russia was oppressive, but the rule of the communists was even more oppressive. Not only were the feudalists and capitalists liquidated (i.e. massacred), but even workers who disagreed suffered the same fate.

It took a long time for communism and socialism, the ideas whose time had come, to be rejected and discarded. A lot of cunning and determination was required in order to reject an accepted idea.

Mikhail Gorbachev and F.W. de Klerk are two of a kind. To get rid of ideas which they believed to be wrong and harmful they had to hide their intentions until they reached the pinnacle of power. Then and then only did they reveal their true feelings about the ideologies they had apparently believed in and propagated in the past. Had they revealed their intentions before they attained supreme power they would have been summarily removed. Their career would have ended as the fanatics would have refused to support their bids for leadership and would have ensured only pure believers would lead.

Using whatever power or influence over the party, the fanatics would have ensured that the heretic would be thrown out and prevented from propagating their heretical ideas. Thus an idea which has outlived its time would go on being practised and would continue to do harm for much longer than it should. Until someone like de Klerk and Gorbachev emerged who were clever enough to hide their ultimate intentions, an idea whose time is over may survive. And the damage that it may cause may continue for long after the people had in their hearts rejected the idea.

This digression is necessary in order to appreciate that an idea whose time has come may not be the ideal that it is made out to be even as it is put into practice. Throughout the history of mankind there had been innumerable ideas which had come, had been accepted as ideal and infallible, only to be found wanting in every way as to be discarded. Feudalism, the divine rights of kings, republicanism, communism, socialism, dictatorship and numerous others are amongst the ideas thrown up by Man in his quest for a perfect system. They all have gone the same way. They are all now in disrepute and have been discarded, to be replaced by new ideas whose time it was said had come.

The nation-state which we are all urged to dismantle in order to make way for globalisation is largely the result of the evolution of tribalism. In Europe, the nation-state realised its peak of sophistication, where loyalty to the country of one's birth entails making the supreme sacrifice for its defence and offence. Such is the loyalty expected of the nationals that even when the country is obviously in the wrong, loyalty is still expected. My country, may it always be right, but my country right or wrong expresses the thinking and attitude of European nationals towards their country.

And so people go to war to defend the nation-state. Throughout the 2,000 years of European history not a year passed without at least one war between the numerous nations of that continent. Nationalism and wars of conquest naturally lead to expansion of states and then to empires. There seems to be no limit to such expansionism. Empires of European states eventually covered the whole globe.

In the years following World War II, which include the Pacific War, the empires came into disrepute and were dismantled. Actually it was the fear of the spread of communist ideology amongst the colonial people which prompted the breakup of European empires outside of Europe.

The lands liberated by the demise of the empires should have reverted to the status quo ante—to tribal territories ruled by different tribes. But the departing imperialist had so successfully implanted the idea of the nation-state that the newly independent peoples opted for the totally foreign concept of nation-states. It was believed that different tribes and races could be made to forget their tribal or racial origins and give their undivided loyalty to the new nation-states whose boundaries had been arbitrarily demarcated by the European colonisers. With tribalism and racial loyalties still very strong it is a wonder that any of the new nation-states survive at all. As it is, many of them are ungovernable.

Intractable tribal and racial wars have become such a feature of these artificially created nation-states that it is quite likely that some will eventually break up. Certainly they would remain unstable and incapable of prospering.

The new nation-states have hardly understood the concept of nationalism and national governments before they are urged to give up their national identities in order to embrace the totally new concept of a global state, for that is what globalisation is all about.

According to the great thinkers and ideologists of the West, globalisation is about breaking down national boundaries as barriers to the flow of capital and goods to wherever they can make the most profit. Since capital and practically all the goods belong to the developed and the rich, the opening of borders must result in the poor having to accept inflows of everything from capital to manufactured goods and even services from the rich.

The result must be massive outflows of whatever foreign exchange the poor countries have.

Still it looked good at first as capital inflows helped the setting up of industries and boosted the local stock market. Jobs were created in large numbers and earnings at all levels increased. The economy grew for some and imports could be paid for. Export-oriented foreign-owned industries helped to earn needed foreign exchange to pay for imports.

Developing countries which accepted the free inflow of capital and goods grew and prospered. Nationalistic countries which had jealously protected their markets were persuaded to open up. Thus Southeast Asia achieved high growth due to the opening up of their countries to foreign capital, goods and services. But certain restrictions were maintained in order to allow local companies to emerge and grow along with the countries' prosperity. Banking in particular was confined largely to nationals.

These minor restrictions coupled with what appeared to be inefficient governments prevented the foreign capitalists from exploiting to the full the potentials and wealth of these countries. They felt that these were irritants which must be got rid off.

Destroying in order to rebuild is of course not a new idea. The phoenix is supposed to rise from its ashes. If prosperity did not result in the newly industrialising middle income countries recognising their faults and taking corrective measures, could not a downturn and economic turmoil awaken them to the need for change and for reforms in their governments and their practices?

Destroying is always easier than building or creating. In this instance it was necessary only to pull out the capital and the economies would collapse. If an inflow of capital could build economies, an outflow, especially a rapid outflow, can be expected to destroy them.

And so borderless capital was pulled out. More than that through currency trading money was devalued so that the countries are left with practically useless money which could pay only for a fraction of the needed imports.

The result was unprecedented: rapid recession and economic turmoil. The people became restless, especially when efficient propaganda machines of the currency and market manipulators convinced them that their problems were due to their governments being corrupt, non-transparent and given to nepotism and cronyism. Accordingly, the people should agitate for reforms which must lead towards opening up the countries to the totally free flows of capital. There should be no more restrictions of any kind. Local considerations must be ignored.

If the governments refuse then they should be overthrown and replaced by governments more willing to adopt the practice of allowing the free flow of capital and goods, i.e. globalisation.

The economies of East Asia were all but destroyed through currency devaluation and stock-market manipulations. Banks were forced to close and those which could remain open suffered runs and became moribund with huge non-performing loans.

The businesses lost market capitalisation as their share prices plummeted and they could not meet margin calls. Deprived of credit their businesses grounded to a standstill. Many went bankrupt and where the IMF had forced open the market, many good businesses and banks were sold literally for a song to foreign predators.

When a currency is devalued and share prices depressed, in terms of foreign currency everything including shares and properties become extremely cheap for foreign buyers. The Malaysian ringgit was devalued by almost 50 per cent which reduced Malaysian shares to half their price in terms of the US dollar. When the share prices went down by 90 per cent, the share value in foreign currency is reduced to 5 per cent of the original value. Thus foreigners with dollars can snap up these formerly good companies for just 5 per cent of their price if they are allowed to.

When businesses fail the government gets no revenue. The government will have to borrow. The IMF will lend but with conditions which will in effect result in total foreign control of the economy. If a country refuses to accept IMF loans and conditions and tries to borrow foreign currency from the market, the rating agencies would downgrade the country's rating so that interest would be so high as to make foreign borrowing suicidal.

All governments subsidise businesses if for nothing else to reduce the cost of living for the people. The IMF directs that subsidies must be removed. At a time when people have lost their jobs and incomes, the removal of subsidies is cruel. But the countries indebted to the IMF must comply or the promised loans would not be made available.

The direct result of the removal of subsidies was to agitate the people and precipitate riots, looting, raping and murder. In the end the government is overthrown and a more compliant government put in place. But the problem is not resolved, certainly not immediately. Instability, inflation and recession continue as the currency traders go on to devalue the currency further.

All these have a very direct connection with the free flow of capital across borders in a globalised economy. Currencies do not devalue themselves. They have no built-in sensors. Governments and currency traders devalue or revalue currencies. Governments devalue currencies in order to help their countries by reducing the costs of goods exported. Governments are not interested in making a profit for themselves through devaluation.

But currency traders devalue currencies for profit. They may claim that they are disciplining governments but they will not discipline governments if they are going to lose money in the process.

Clearly, the currency traders and the stock-market manipulators are unscrupulous. They don't care about the social cost incurred and the poverty and misery they cause. Since globalisation affords them the opportunity to exploit, they will exploit. And we have seen how their exploitation results in financial and economic turmoil and in political upheavals all over the world.

Has the world economy gained by their exploitation of the globalised market? They have no doubt brought prosperity for their own countries. But everywhere else throughout the whole world they have caused economic turmoil and regression, and the destruction of the wealth which had taken decades to build. World trade is badly disrupted, affecting even the wealthy developed countries. Truly the poverty they cause is very many times greater than the profits they make and the wealth they bring to their own countries. It is worse than a zero-sum game. The wealth of whole nations is destroyed in order to give a little profit to a few people.

Admittedly, the economies of East Asia are now showing signs of recovery. But this is due to the currency traders and the shortselling manipulators being curbed. Their greed and excesses which caused the LTCM disaster have resulted in banks denying funds for their activities. At the same time there was a fear that if they were not curbed then the countries affected might take action by regaining control over their currencies or merely refusing to pay their debts. The recovery of the economies of East Asia is not even due to the loans extended to them by the IMF. It must be noted that these loans are largely for paying the loans due to foreign banks.

The experience of East Asian developing countries is that the free flow of capital across their borders can result not just in economic wellbeing but can actually destroy their economies. The destruction is actually far greater than the contribution to growth. What had taken decades to build can be destroyed in a matter of days or weeks. The subsequent turmoil far exceeds the benefit of the inflows of capital.

It must be admitted that foreign capital invested in permanent industries are not harmful. They cannot easily liquidate and take out their money. It is the short-term investments in stocks and shares which can do massive damage. They can be suddenly liquidated and the money pulled out. Of course, the currency traders invest in nothing at all. They merely do shortselling of currencies which they borrow in order to devalue them and make billions overnight.

If free capital flows and currency trading are manifestations of a borderless globalised world, is there any reason why the developing countries should accept globalisation unquestioningly? The risk and the destruction are simply too great for them. Rescue operations by the international agencies can saddle them with more debts which they may never be able to repay. Rebuilding their economies would take decades. Placed under the supervision of the international agencies they would lose control over their economy. And as can be seen in some cases even their politics can come under the control and manipulation of foreigners. Globalisation can therefore result in loss of economic, political and social independence. This is too high a price to pay for the dubious benefit of gaining access to the markets of the rich for goods which they do not produce.

Besides, the markets of the rich are easily closed by other means, e.g. by raising standards to a level the poor countries cannot meet. As for their raw materials the prices can be manipulated very easily. For decades now increasing amounts of raw materials and commodities have to be sold to buy less and less of the manufactured goods of the rich. The terms of trade have consistently been in favour of the rich.

Globalisation can bring benefits but only if it is given a human face, if it is governed by rules and practices which can ensure that the poor countries will not be faced with repeated economic turmoil and regression. It is entirely possible for this to be done. But it can only be done if the international community, including the poor, are given a say in the interpretation of globalisation. Currently the poor have hardly any say. Many who are obliged to the rich for aid and loans are not able to speak out.

The first thing that everyone must admit is that a level playing field is not enough. The players must at least be of the same size. If that is not possible then handicaps must be given to the disadvantaged. It has always been so in sports and there is no reason why it cannot be in international competition where the competitors are even less evenly matched.

Secondly, in order to have free trade we must regulate. We have to discard some regulations but they must be replaced with new ones worked out by the international community and enforced by truly independent international agencies, not the ones which are under the control of the rich and the powerful.

There must be transparency in trade and dealings between nations. No one, certainly not the currency traders and market manipulators, should be exempted from the requirement to open their books. There must be limit-up or limit-down provisions so as to prevent excesses.

Loans extended by banks must be prudent and balanced. If countries are subjected to ratings so must the hedge funds. They may not leverage by more than a reasonable multiple of their assets. And those competing with them as well as the governments must be able to leverage by the same multiple at reasonable rates.

Ratings must be done by international non-profit organisations financed by the international community. No one should dominate through too high a proportion of the financing.

There must be a tax on all international speculators. They may not operate out of offshore financial centres. The tax must be shared so as to help the countries ravaged by them to recover.

These are some of the things that can help give a human face to globalisation. There must be many more things that can be done which can make globalisation more welcome by all, including the poor.

Globalisation, a borderless world, is already a fact. In the field of information distribution and e-commerce, borders mean very little now. But the fact that globalisation has come (and is apparently irresistible) does not mean we should just sit by and watch as the predators destroy us.

Those of us who believe in sharing, in prospering our neighbours, we certainly cannot just submit. Many of us still remember the days of colonial subjugation, the pain and the humility. Many still beat the scars of the unequal battles for our independence. We fought for hundreds of years. We have only just won. We have hardly tasted the fruits of our sacrifices. We cannot now be forced to submit to foreign domination once again. It may not be the raw colonialisation that we knew but it is not too far different.

We must therefore work to put a human face to globalisation. As during our struggle for independence, there are many amongst the rich who are with us, who appreciate our views. Let them join up and be counted. Let them join us in our new struggle to preserve our self-respect and our rights.

I am not being rhetorical. I am not overreacting. I am not being alarmist. We in Malaysia have been through two terrible years fighting shadowy predators. We have barely survived. I wouldn't like to see friends going through what we went through.

I have merely tried to give a true picture of what globalisation can mean if present interpretations are accepted unquestioningly.

14

Globalisation and the Borderless World

"Globalisation and a borderless world seem very attractive in this Information Age and advances in transportation and communication. We now live in a global village. We will all be citizens of the Planet Earth. But apparently we are not going to be equal citizens."

WE ARE NOW at a crucial moment in history. We are now at the threshold of a new century and a new millennium. If what is happening to the world today is any indication, the new century is going to bring a lot of challenges for us in the developing countries. We must therefore take stock of things and

---

A speech delivered at the 9th Summit of the G15 in Montego Bay, Jamaica, on February 10, 1999

examine the trends and the systems which are being foisted on us in a unipolar world.

First, the unipolar world itself. We had welcomed the end of the Cold War believing that peace and freedom would now be ours. But unfortunately we find that losing the option to defect to the other side has deprived us of the little leverage that we had in defending our interests.

The defeat of communism and socialism means that only one politico-economic creed is allowed. When communism and socialism were contesting with capitalism, the latter modified itself in order to be more acceptable. Today capitalism finds little need to compete for acceptance. As a result the worst aspects of the system have been bared. Anything done in the name of capitalism must be accepted on pain of being labelled a heretic.

In East Asia we experienced the new capitalism in the form of the free flow of capital across our borders. We had welcomed foreign capital in order to boost our growth. We still do but now we realise the damage to our economy when that capital is suddenly withdrawn. From being miracle economies we have now become impoverished nations.

The great Asian tigers are now no more. Reduced to whimpering and begging, they are but a shadow of their former selves. Their people are starving, rioting and looting. Their governments have been overthrown and their political system so undermined that they cannot govern effectively. They have to accept foreign direction of their internal affairs.

But the assault on them is far from over. Whether it is planned or not their impoverishment has exposed them to the danger of losing their independence. A condition for getting aid from such institutions as the IMF is to open up their economies to unrestricted penetration by foreign businesses. They may not protect their indigenous banks and industries. These may be taken over or shouldered aside by foreign giants.

As if the foreign corporations are not big enough, they are now engaged in consolidating themselves. Banks and industries in the developed countries are merging into super-big entities, each bigger than the developing countries. When these super-big giants move in, their local counterparts will just suffocate to death.

I am sure it is not their intention to interfere in local politics but we know that in banana republics the managers of banana plantations wield more power than the Presidents of these countries. The temptation to interfere in local politics might be too much for the foreign giants to resist.

Globalisation and a borderless world seem very attractive in this Information Age and advances in transportation and communication. We now live in a global village. We will all be citizens of the Planet Earth. But apparently we are not going to be equal citizens.

While borderlessness is being interpreted as the right of capital to flow anywhere unconditionally, the poor people may not cross borders into rich countries with equal freedom. For them the barb wire fences and the border guards will remain.

Even as globalisation is being promoted, the powerful are actively increasing the traditional basis of power i.e military strength. The defeat of the communists was initially thought to end the arms race. But the quest for ever more destructive weapons have not abated. Huge sums are spent on research into destructive weapons and equipping vast armies in the use of these weapons.

To recover the money spent, the poor countries are persuaded to buy ever more sophisticated weapons. The result is not only tension and minor arms races but misallocation of their limited funds. Less is being spent on the well-being of society.

While misbehaviour on the part of the weak may attract rockets and bombs, the massive violations of human rights in such places as Bosnia-Herzegovina and Kosovo, go on with impunity.

Power not only corrupts but it must also be free of any challenge. If anyone has the temerity to criticise those with power, the result can be very painful for the critic. Every weapon at the disposal of the power will be employed maximally against the critic.

Amongst these weapons is the media. If anyone criticises the actions of the mighty the media will demonise the critic and cause him to lose credibility. That way the abusers of power will remain free to continue their abuses.

We are a group of 16 countries scattered over three continents. We are weak. We are poor. And we are linked with each other only by thin and friable beliefs that we have something in common, that we have common problems, that we need to cooperate to enhance the little strength that we have and to use it to enable us to survive. I must say in all these we are not succeeding too well.

On the other hand, the rich and the powerful are consolidating, forming powerful cohesive politico-economic alliances. They meet, they plan and they execute strategies impacting on the world. Clearly, if we want to safeguard our future we have to be aware of the forces around us, to consult with each other more often and to have a common stand on most issues.

I have painted a very gloomy picture of the future, of the new century and the new millennium. Maybe I am over pessimistic. Maybe I am exaggerating. I have been wrong before and I may be wrong again. But I was right many times also and it is possible that I will be right again this time, if not fully at least partly. And if I am partly right even, it is not going to be good for us in the developing world. We may find our newly won independence eroded away.

Malaysians took four centuries to liberate themselves. We have been independent just for 41 years. We do not relish losing that independence. Just as we struggled hard to gain independence we will struggle equally hard or harder to retain it.

We have not just seen the signs but we are actually going through a painful experience of the kind of world the future will bring. For the time being we have been able to retain our freedom but we are not sure that we can successfully fend off future challenges.

Paradoxically the greatest catastrophe for us who had always been anti-communist is the defeat of communism. The end of the Cold War between East and West has deprived us of the only leverage we had, the option to defect. Now we can turn to no one.

As a member of the G15 I feel a need to shout my warnings. I know I will be ridiculed but that is a small price to pay. The world may not see a clash of civilisations but the disparities between the weak and the strong is such that might will continue to be regarded as right.

I do not ask to be believed. But I do appreciate this opportunity to speak out before you, the leaders of middle-income developing countries. When I condemned the currency traders at the height of their attack on the East Asian countries I was punished by having the currency of my country devalued further. I was told to cease and desist. I did not and the currency and the stock market and the image of Malaysia suffered. What I have said today may attract other punitive actions.

That is a risk we will have to take. But I have to say what I have to say. I hope this Summit will result in a greater understanding of the problems which lie ahead and greater collaboration between us.

15

Restoring Confidence, Regenerating Growth: Managing Globalisation Better

"Globalisation can bring about a better world if we are not fanatical about it. Not everything that is done in the name of globalisation will give good results. We should always be on the lookout for adverse consequences and be prepared to take corrective actions or even to reverse certain globalisation trends in order to ensure that these adverse consequences will not befall us."

AS we approach a new millennium, it is imperative that we devise and put in place a better economic and financial regime (now referred to as architecture) for the world. Some of these will be the result of technological progress but others will reflect the emergence of new commercial and sociological ideas and values. With your indulgence, I would like to take this opportunity to

A speech delivered at the APEC Business Summit 1998 in Kuala Lumpur, Malaysia, on November 15, 1998

discuss the present architecture (or the lack thereof) as manifested by the anarchical and unregulated capital flows in the international monetary system. In doing so we must not be tied down by fanatical beliefs which act as mental blocks to our recognition of the facts involved.

What are the facts?

Firstly, before July 1997, before the Thai baht came under attack and was devalued, the countries of East Asia were all prosperous. Such was their prosperity that they were described as economic tigers and dragons. Their prosperity was not just confined to a privileged few although these privileged few did exist. Their prosperity was very well distributed. They were successful in reducing poverty to below 20 per cent of their population. Malaysia had reduced this to below 7 per cent. Their per capita incomes had increased from the level of least developed countries to the middle-income group. For developing countries their infrastructure was far superior to those of other developing countries. Unemployment rates were very low so much so that workers from other region flock in to share the prosperity.

Their governments were not the best in the world but despite obvious cases of cronyism, etc, they must have been doing something right to prosper their countries. They were largely stable. Social and political unrests were minimal.

This was the situation in the countries of East Asia. But by July 1997 the dragon economies of East Asia were collapsing one after another. What happened? The governments were the same. They had not changed policies or systems. The people were peaceful and were working as hard as ever. There was no revolution or civil war or even street demonstrations.

Despite everything remaining the same they all suddenly experienced economic turmoil. Their banks and businesses collapsed. Millions of workers lost their jobs. There was not enough food, medicine or milk for the children. Civil unrest and street demos with looting and even killings and rape became common. And governments were overthrown.

What triggered all these upheavals was the rapid devaluation of the currencies of these countries. And alongside this came the collapse of the stock market.

Ever since the Bretton Woods fixed exchange rate regime was abandoned the exchange rates of currencies had never been stable. Businessmen had to hedge against exchange rate changes and business went on without too much difficulty. But when the exchange rate changes became violent, rapid and unpredictable, business was affected. In one case, the fall in the value of the currency was 600 per cent, i.e. you require six times the amount of local currency in order to pay for whatever it is you want to import.

Admittedly currency devaluation has different effects on different people. For exporters of Malaysian palm oil the earnings and profits increased because the sale was priced in US dollars. For importers the cost of goods increased resulting in higher prices at home. For those who import components to add value and re-export, the blessings were mixed.

Businesses and banks can go bankrupt very easily as loans and loan repayments became inflated greatly. Indeed many banks and businesses closed down, resulting in unemployment. The cost of living rises, resulting in demands for higher wages. Eventually there would be strikes and riots if the government fails to provide relief. But the government also finds its revenue decreasing as corporate taxes shrink. The net effect is to impoverish the country and the people.

It was suggested that the economy would recover if financial reforms are carried out, if governments are less corrupt, etc. But those countries which tried to conform have found that reforms have not made things any better. In fact, the economic turmoil worsened despite the reforms and the loans from the IMF. There are attempts to paint a happy picture of economies under the IMF recovering. But the facts belie this. The people in these countries are still suffering unemployment and shortages of food and other goods. None of the currencies of these countries have regained their previous strength.

In any case, if they recover there is no guarantee they will not be attacked again by the currency traders and the share-market raiders. Several Latin American countries have been attacked repeatedly with grievous results despite their reforms. The fact is that currency traders attack not because the governments or the systems are bad but because they see opportunities for making money for themselves. An impoverished country offers them no such opportunity, but a middle income country would have sufficient money to yield a good return for them but would not be strong enough to take countermeasures.

Allegations about bad governments, etc, are just excuses. For currency traders it is the profits to be made that influence their decisions to attack the currency. There is one word for this: greed.

It is said that currency trading is 20 times the value of world trade. We all know that world trade is economically beneficial to every country. Jobs are created, industries flourish, land, sea and transportation and all kinds of businesses are generated because of world trade. There is probably not a single person in the world who does not gain something from world trade. It is reasonable to expect that if world trade is increased by 20 times, then the whole world and everyone on earth would be greatly enriched.

But what is there to show for the huge trade in currency, 20 times bigger than world trade? The number of people who invest in the hedge funds and the banks are very small—thousands perhaps as against a world population of six billion. These people are rich people who can live comfortably without the profits from currency trading. In contrast, tens of millions of poor workers lose their jobs and are starving because of currency trading, not to mention the loss of wealth of many developing countries which run into hundreds of billions.

There was no currency trading as such several decades ago and the world's economy did not do badly. Indeed the world's economies were more prosperous. If there is no currency trading now, the world's economy would not collapse. Nobody would really suffer.

We need to change money for the purpose of trading. We need to determine how many units of one currency is equal to how many units of another currency, i.e. the exchange rates. But we need not leave it to the currency traders to determine the rate. Various indices can be used and governments can agree to a reasonable exchange rate. It may be difficult but it is not impossible.

There are many mechanisms for determining the exchange rates which can be devised by the fertile minds of economists and financiers. Governments of powerful countries just cannot abdicate their roles in determining the exchange-rate mechanism. They owe it to their peoples and their countries to accept the responsibility of determining the exchange rate.

The excuse they give that currency trading cannot be made transparent is ridiculous. On the one hand, the currency traders condemned governments for their lack of transparency, and on the other hand, these self-appointed discipliners of governments are themselves not transparent. Despite dealing in billions and trillions of dollars we do not know who they are, how they trade, where they trade and who invests with them. It is only when they fail (as exemplified by the collapse of the LTCM Fund) that we learn about them and their massive trading.

It is shocking to learn that with a capital of four billion the Fund could borrow up to one trillion dollars, 250 times more. Banks are supposed to exercise prudence. Is this what is meant by banking prudence? Aren't the governments supposed to supervise banks or have they abdicated this role also?

While nothing was done to stop such banking imprudence, rich governments were quick to act to bail out the hedge funds, using money deposited in the banks by ordinary people. The rich investors in the hedge funds are being bailed out with money belonging to poor people. Yet the same governments condemn any bailout of corporations belonging to the public using public funds. Such inconsistency and double-standards are glaring.

The Malaysian economy is minute compared to the world's economy. If there is no Malaysia the world's economy will not collapse. We cannot do anything to affect the world's economy adversely or otherwise. We are just too insignificant. Hence the furore over Malaysia's decision to stop the ringgit from being traded by the currency traders is quite unreasonable.

We have not hurt anyone, except the currency traders. Even then only minimally because the ringgit is only a small fragment of the huge trillion-dollar trading that the currency traders are involved in. No one else is affected by the government declaring that offshore ringgit would cease to be legal tender unless they are returned to the country a month after the new policy was announced. The owners of offshore ringgit would continue to own them within the country where they can earn interest or be profitably invested.

Other than this all business transactions are unaffected by the action taken by the Malaysian government. All imports and exports must be paid in foreign currencies. There is nothing new in this as all foreigners convert the ringgit into their currencies when they receive payment. Now they don't have to convert as the local importer will convert the ringgit locally in order to pay for his imports. Malaysian exporters will be paid in foreign currency which they can convert to ringgit within the country. This arrangement has not caused any problem. In fact, Malaysian trade is as active as ever. In the two months of the so-called capital control Malaysia registered a trade surplus of over RM6 billion.

Within the country only the ringgit is used. The exchange rate with the US dollar is fixed at RM3.80 to US$1. The exchange rates between the US dollar and other currencies are used to determine the ringgit exchange rate with these currencies. Since these exchange rates move, the ringgit exchange rate with other currencies also move. But as 70 per cent of Malaysian trade is done in US dollar, the variable rates of exchange of the US dollar against other currencies do not affect Malaysian trade much.

As the US dollar weakens against other currencies, the ringgit will also weaken. We are now about 7 per cent weaker as compared to our neighbours. That simply makes us more competitive. We need not change the exchange rate unless it is too weak or too strong compared to our competitors. Alternatively, our competitors can weaken their currencies or strengthen them according to their competitive needs.

163

The other leg of the currency control has to do with the inflow and outflow of short-term capital into the share market. By requiring the capital invested to stay in the country for one year we hope to prevent short-selling. Speculators will not like this but again the Malaysian portfolio is minute by comparison to their world-wide operations. So it would not affect their money-making operations very much.

I am emphasising the smallness of the Malaysian market simply because many great economic and financial minds seem to think that we have done something that can damage the process of liberalisation and global-isation of the world financial system. We cannot. We are too small. Why not leave Malaysia alone with its idiosyn-crasies. If we are wrong then we will pay the price. It would serve us right. But the world community would have learnt something and be better off for it.

The reason for Malaysia removing the ringgit out of the reach of the currency traders is because we still be-lieve that currency traders are too powerful and com-pletely irresponsible. They don't mind bankrupting countries and regions, impoverishing millions of work-ers and destroying whole economies in their quest for profits. We had asked the world to regulate the currency traders but we were laughed at for not understanding the world's financial system, for being in denial, for prof-ligate ways, for building the world's highest building, etc.

Now the world is beginning to realise that the activi-ties of the currency traders can adversely affect them also. And they have called for some studies. From past experience we know they are going to take a long time. And when they decide it could possibly be only to their benefit. The developing countries cannot hope for a re-gime that can save them especially as they will not be involved in the formulation of that regime. The last time the G7 decided to correct the imbalance in their trade with Japan, they revalued the yen, suddenly pushing up the debts of developing countries by two and a half times. Already the G7 is talking about using the IMF to get the developing countries to accept the IMF, i.e. developed countries guidelines.

Malaysia cannot wait for this process, for the ponderous movements of the great powers. Unless they see their own collapse staring them in the eyes, and they saw this when the LTCM failed, they would not do anything. By the time they decide, it would have been curtains for Malaysia.

But we are being urged to reverse our decision. Some say it is wrong while others say we have already achieved our objective and we should go back now. But we are of the view that there is still anarchy in the international financial market. If we go back, there is no guarantee that we would not be attacked again.

Again I would like to restate that we are not doing anyone any real harm. So leave us to our devices. It would serve us right if we fail.

Our currency control will remain in place for as long as the world refuses to bring order to the financial market. There is a lot of contradictions between what the world says it believes in and what it does. We are constantly being told to abide by the rule of law. Presently the world believes in laws, i.e. in rules and regulations to govern the behaviour of everyone. Yet we are being told also that we must deregulate, we must leave finance and trade to market forces. Which one do we follow? Bill Gates used his great financial power to build up his business. He is a true free marketeer. But the US government thinks he is being unfair to his competitors. We see no difference between Bill Gates and currency traders. Why should Microsoft be penalised for using market forces when currency traders are not?

In currency trading the hedge funds are the Bill Gates of the international financial market. They compete against puny central banks of developing countries. The central banks have no chance at all, especially against the combined financial strength of all the funds and the banks which lend them money. If it is unfair, improper and illegal for Bill Gates to corner the market then shouldn't the activities of the funds be considered unfair also? If Bill Gates' competitors have to be protected should we not protect the victims of the hedge funds also?

I have dwelled at length on currency trading. You are of course not currency traders. In fact, you may not be affected much by currency trading. But there cannot be prosperity for anyone if an activity that causes the impoverishment of a quarter of the world is not reined in.

Malaysia believes in prospering its neighbours, far and near. It is not charity which motivates us. It is what we prefer to describe as enlightened self-interest. When Malaysia became prosperous because of Japanese investments, we became a good market for Japanese goods. So the Japanese reaped double benefit from their investments here.

If, on the other hand, you cause a country to become poor you will lose a market. And with that you will become poorer yourself.

East Asia was a huge market for the products of Europe and America. Much of that capacity to buy has now been lost. This will show up in the trade figures of the rich countries. They may not be impoverished to the same extent, but they will not prosper as much as they used to.

Today we are seeing that the whole world is becoming adversely affected by currency trading. Getting the world back on its economic feet is going to be extremely difficult. It will take a long time.

A world that is poor is no good to the business community. An APEC region that is largely poor will not be good for the economies of Asia-Pacific or the rest of the world.

We are rushing onward towards globalisation simply because we cannot isolate ourselves from each other any more. There is nothing that is so inherently good that it cannot be abused to deliver what is bad. Democracy, for example, is good but some democratic countries seem never able to have a viable government. All the great religions of the world are good, but their adherents fight and kill each other despite being urged to be brothers. Globalisation too is good but it can be abused, abused in such a way that instead of worldwide prosperity there will be worldwide poverty or extreme disparities between rich and poor, international and civil disorders, revolts, rebellion and all kinds of crises.

Globalisation can bring about a better world if we are not fanatical about it. Not everything that is done in the name of globalisation will give good results. We should always be on the lookout for adverse consequences and be prepared to take corrective actions or even to reverse certain globalisation trends in order to ensure that these adverse consequences will not befall us.

Currency speculation and the rapid flow of investment capital in and out of countries may be compatible with globalisation. But we have seen how much harm they can do to the economies of the developing countries. When we see these things we must be prepared to take corrective measures to reverse the process. It is not the system that has to be adhered to. It is the results which count. If the results are good, by all means embrace the particular manifestation of globalisation. If, on the other hand, the results are bad, and in the case of currency trading they are bad, then we should reexamine the system and be prepared to jettison that expression of the system.

We must proceed cautiously with globalisation. The countries of APEC are not equally developed. Any competition between them will not be fair competition even if the playing fields are level. Handicaps must be given so that weaknesses can be compensated.

When an economy feels that it is not going to be overwhelmed by the massive strength of a competitor, when an economy's handicap is recognised and compensated for, then there will be confidence and a willingness to open up. Growth can then take place and regeneration made possible.

We should not reject globalisation. It is coming. It has to come to this shrinking world. But the big and the powerful can be magnanimous and accord the small and the weak time and latitude to prepare and to make adjustments.

Creative destruction is not the way. We can build on what we have instead of destroying and expecting the phoenix to rise from its ashes. It may not rise at all or it may take too long a time.

APEC is a segment of the global community. It can provide a model for the regeneration of the global village. We are going through difficult times and we need the lessons of experience. The East Asian members of APEC can provide the experience and we all can help devise the right formula to restore confidence, regenerate growth and manage globalisation better.

16

Globalisation: Colonialism Revisited

"... After 50 years of being free, largely on account of the Eastern and Western blocs confronting each other, our freedom is being eroded and colonialism is coming back. Of course, it is not going to assume the same forms but it is colonialism all the same."

GIVEN THE IMPORTANCE of the issue of apartheid in the context of NAM and the role that this movement played towards its elimination, this meeting in Durban is of particular significance for NAM. NAM rejoiced when South Africa was freed from the odious apartheid regime and achieved majority

A speech delivered at the 12th Conference of the Heads of State or Government of the Non-Aligned Movement (NAM) Countries in Durban, South Africa, on September 2, 1998

rule. It is therefore most fitting that President Nelson Mandela, the living symbol of the epic struggle to end apartheid, has now taken over the mantle of leadership of NAM. South Africa had for long been at the core of NAM's effort to uphold the cherished principles of freedom, justice and equality. This long association, coupled with its active role in the movement, strengthens our confidence in South Africa's qualification to lead NAM into the new millennium.

When NAM was founded in 1961, the world was divided into two blocs, into Eastern and Western camps, into communists and non-communists. It was an unstable world, with the nuclear powers accumulating the weapons of mass destruction sufficient to blow up the world. It was a world perpetually on the brink of war. We in the third world lived in a constant state of trepidation and fear.

We thus felt a need to come together to protect our recently gained independence, our hopes and aspirations. We did not want to be aligned with any of the blocs but to retain our freedom of choice, our own systems of government, our rights as sovereign nations. In this, we felt we could succeed because we were in many instances being wooed by both East and West. We had the option to align ourselves with one or the other. And that option forced the two blocs to treat us with a modicum of consideration. Both were ready to extend help, aid, loans, gifts, etc. Their courting enabled us to retain our precious independence. We were, I believe, a little bit spoilt because of the courting.

Then the Eastern bloc decided to throw in the towel. They surrendered unconditionally and a bipolar world became a unipolar one overnight. Some of us liked to believe that the more humane and righteous bloc won. Dictatorships were out and enlightened democracy apparently triumphed. We would surely be seeing a better world, a world where human rights are respected, where the rule of law prevails, internationally and nationally. We would see a world of independent countries exercising their rights freely.

But I think we were wrong. The loss of the option to defect has exposed us to threats from which we find nowhere to hide. We have to submit or we would be bludgeoned into submission. We have seen ample demonstrations of the kind of things that can happen to those who fail to submit. I will not elaborate but suffice to say that we and our people, innocent or otherwise, are no longer safe. An eye for an eye is said to be the basis of Muslim justice, but for the vengeful powers one eye is not sufficient. Two or more eyes can be exacted for the loss of one. It does not matter if the eyes belong to the innocent. The important thing is to teach the world a lesson. Submit or be damned.

But physical assault is not the only weapon of the powerful. A new weapon has been found which is even more effective. Merely by devaluing the currency of a nation and so impoverishing it, submission can be obtained even from the proudest and the most independent of nations.

The highly successful dragons and tigers of East Asia have now realised how flimsy their great economies are. They had thought that their mastery of industrial technologies and management skills would enable them to grow into developed nations, able to compete in the marketplace with the most developed nations of the Western bloc. But in a matter of months their decades of achievements have been destroyed and they are reduced to begging for help.

When we achieved independence, the world believed in the sovereignty of nation-states. Proudly we maintained that our internal affairs and policies are ours to determine. Our former colonial masters should leave us alone. While the Cold War lasted, they did. But once the Cold War was over, the triumphant victors began to enunciate new concepts of international relations which could give them back their dominant imperial role.

After the Gulf War demonstrated that there is indeed now only one power, a new concept of international relations was introduced. Briefly, no country is sovereign if that country is judged by the Western bloc to have breached their norms of correct behaviour. Initially, violation of human rights is expected to warrant interference in the internal affairs of independent nations. Very quickly the right to interfere extended to political and economic systems or policies.

Now, every nation must adopt the so-called free and open-market system which will enable the rich and avaricious capitalists of the Western nations to enter and leave any country at will. They can own and set up banks and businesses everywhere and anywhere unfettered by the national needs and aspirations of any nation. They must be free to revalue and devalue currencies and shares unimpeded by government rules, laws and regulations. They will control and determine the exchange rates of all currencies anywhere, anytime. But the world must not know who they are and how they work. While they require governments to be open and transparent, they themselves will remain shadowy and their operations closed to inspection.

The countries of the world have two choices: submit or be impoverished by having their currencies devalued and their stock markets destroyed. Unfortunately, whether they submit or not, the result is the same. From being stable and prosperous they will now become poverty-stricken and beset with political and social turmoil. Today, more than 25 million workers in the countries attacked by these capitalists have lost their jobs. This means that they have no food, no medicine and no milk for their children. For this the blame is put squarely on the governments of these countries for not providing a safety net in the form of unemployment benefits. That the practice in Asia of providing lifetime employment is not considered good for the workers. According to Western belief, workers should be sacked or retrenched if the business is not doing well and the government will support them. Sackings and uncertainty of employment is considered better than guarantee of lifetime employment. And so millions of workers in East Asia are now unemployed because the countries are being forced to accept the so-called superior Western practices.

With tens of thousands of businesses and scores of banks folding up, governments are now without adequate revenue to pay wages and fund public works. The loans they have been forced to take will ensure that for decades to come they will be debt slaves to the rich in the world.

That the free flow of capital and the right of speculators to determine the exchange rates of currencies have clearly destroyed many vibrant economies, resulting in chaos and extreme poverty, have not resulted in any second thoughts on the rightfulness of the free-market system, of unregulated capitalism and the free flow of capital across borders. Instead, the economic recession and its attendant repercussions are blamed on the governments. The market forces are merely disciplining governments so that they will adopt superior Western ways of governance and economic management.

The protests of the victims are not only ignored but they are actually censored by the international media controlled by the West. Apparently freedom of speech and the press is not for everyone. And so the capitalists of the West continue to revel in the ease with which they can strip the wealth of the world. Their raids and attacks have become more frequent and more widespread. Even the former bastion of socialism/communism, the Eastern bloc, are not free from them.

Logically, globalisation and a borderless world should mean not just a free flow of capital across borders but also of people. Yet the proponents of a borderless world object strongly to the free flow of people into their countries. Actual fences are being erected so as to stop the people from poor countries from coming in. Those who manage to overcome the physical barriers are subject to physical abuses and forced to recross the borders. In fact, those who profess religions which are not approved are subject to ethnic cleansing and forced out of their own countries.

Again we see double standards at work here. While globalisation is interpreted as the free flow of capital and goods from rich countries to poor countries, the free flow of people across borders into rich countries is not considered consistent with borderlessness and globalisation.

The tendency of the rich and powerful to interpret everything to their advantage is not confined to countering alleged terrorism and the markets of the world. It extends into ideology and systems of decision-making and governments. Thus the world is being told and indeed being pressured into the acceptance of liberal democracy and the will of the majority. Those who fail to accept democratic practices of the most liberal kind are subjected to harassments, sanctions, bad-mouthing by the media and a variety of threats and pressures. That such acts are actually undemocratic do not bother the liberal democrats of the first world. Thus leaders of independent nations are kidnapped and tried under laws which they never subscribed to, harbours are mined and economic sanctions applied unilaterally.

Yet in the United Nations there is not the slightest semblance of democracy. Anyone of five countries can veto the will of the majority; in fact, they can do anything they like in the name of the organisation simply because they won a war fifty years ago. And so one country can reject the will of six billion inhabitants of this planet while demanding that other countries accept liberal democracy. They see no contradiction in their stand.

The interpretations of the United Nations' Resolutions have been appropriated by a few powers in the United Nations Security Council. The United Nations General Assembly is totally ignored and bypassed. And so the United Nations' Resolutions in favour of their proteges are upheld while those in favour of the countries not categorised as their clients are either misinterpreted or ignored.

The United Nations is a great concept but it was formed by an exclusive club of nations who presumed they had a monopoly of the right to determine the shape of this world forever because they won World War II. It was an example of justice according to the victors. Such justice is obviously biased. But, nevertheless, they will resist any reform of the United Nations which might impinge upon their right to use the United Nations to legitimise their national policies. Democratic processes are no argument for them to change their stance. They and in particular the most powerful amongst them will do just what they like in the furtherance of their national policies.

Those amongst us who entertain hopes of democratic reforms in the United Nations should give up our dreams. We are not going to see anything like the reforms we envisage. If there is to be any reform it is only going to strengthen the hands of those who are already strong and who want more power for themselves.

The fact is that after fifty years of being free, largely on account of the Eastern and Western blocs confronting each other, our freedom is being eroded and colonialism is coming back. Of course, it is not going to assume the same form, but it is colonialism all the same. The strong and the mighty will quite literally rule us, determine our fate and our roles in the international scheme of things. Poor as we are we will be exploited even as in the past they exploited us.

Our only hope lies in staying together. The relevance of being non-aligned in a unipolar world may be questioned. But there are any number of reasons for us to stay together. Divided, we will succumb, but in unity there is a chance that we will survive and possibly retain our integrity and independence.

NAM is therefore worth saving and rejuvenating. After our meeting in Belgrade, a small group made up of 15 non-aligned nations was set up to experiment with South-South Cooperation. It is not a resounding success. Not every country is dedicated to South-South Cooperation. But the *modus operandi* of cooperation between the countries of the South have been devised and tried out quite successfully. It is perhaps time for truly interested members of NAM to be brought into the scheme so that apart from our tri-yearly meet, we can have mutually beneficial interactions. Since the founding of the G15, trade between them has expanded by almost 400 per cent. With greater effort trade can be really substantial.

Clearly, NAM is still a useful forum and organisation for the countries unwilling to be mere clients of the first world. It was founded in a bipolar world but it is clearly still needed in a unipolar world. The need to defend our rights is greater than ever. None of us can do it alone but together we stand a better chance.

We now know that the weapons to be used against us are not just military force but also economic forces. The assaults through economic forces are more subtle but are no less damaging and effective compared to military assaults. We need to know about the economic forces that may be used and how we may defend ourselves. As with the struggle against colonisation, the time may come when the good elements amongst the powerful will see the injustice of their ways and throw their weight behind us. It may take a long time as indeed colonialism took a long time to be condemned. But God willing, the day will come when justice will triumph. Until then let us keep NAM alive and let us do what we can for ourselves.

17

Governance, Smart Partnership and Unfettered Globalisation

"Globalisation ... must be interpreted correctly if it is ever going to bring about a better life for everyone in this world. Presently we are not too convinced that it is going to be good for us in the developing world. We have seen how the free flow of capital has damaged our economies and we fear that globalisation may turn out to be like socialism or communism, ideas which were touted for a time and were then discarded as wrong."

AT THE FIRST Southern Africa International Dialogue, I spoke of globalisation, its inevitability and its challenges. I spoke of the possible social and economic injustice that can result from unfettered globalisation where the interest of the strongest reigns supreme. Finally, I spoke of the need for develop-

A speech delivered at the 2th Southern Africa International Dialogue (SAID) on Smart Partnership in Swakopmund, Namibia, on July 28, 1998

ing nations to present a united front and to form smart partnerships to face these challenges. This need has become very acute for the developing world is now under siege.

When I mentioned all those things at the first Southern Africa International Dialogue, I had no inkling of the economic catastrophe that was soon to befall my country and the other countries of prosperous dynamic Southeast Asia. I had every faith in the milk of human kindness, in the belief that in this day and age the exploitation of the poor by the rich is a thing of the past and our modern civilisation would not allow it to come back. Now I know otherwise.

I am not a racist; neither am I anti-White nor anti-European, but I cannot help but notice that ethnic Europeans have an infinite capacity to convince themselves that, whatever it is that they are doing at the moment, it is right, proper and just. Thus, when they were colonising us, exploiting our wealth in Asia, Africa and the Americas, even warring and killing us, they were able to convince themselves that it was a burden imposed on them by God, a cross that they must bear for what they were doing was to civilise the natives and to bring culture and religion to them. They called it the White Man's Burden. If in the process the natives were oppressed it was incidental and quite unavoidable.

In their own countries their capitalists exploited the working classes. They believed it was right because they were using their capital and their industries to create jobs for the miserably poor. The working classes knew no better. Left to themselves they would starve or resort to crime.

Their working classes revolted, and influenced by economic and political theories, they adopted socialist and communist ideologies. Again they were convinced completely of the justice and the righteousness of their ideologies. And being convinced they were prepared to fight and kill in order to achieve their objectives. The hated capitalists were exterminated in order to set up communist republics of the workers. Elsewhere the socialists banded together, initiated strikes, disrupted the capitalist economies, set up workers and socialist parties and grabbed power. In Germany the infamous Nazis (or National Socialist) used terrorism in order to seize power and set up a dictatorship, completely convinced that Aryan domination of the world was their destiny.

The communists and the socialists were absolutely convinced that they had the formula for human salvation. What could be more fair and just than to give everyone an equal share of the wealth of the nation? If in the course of doing so people were killed or oppressed or otherwise terrorised, that could not be helped. The main thing was that their way and objectives were right.

And so country after country were forced in one way or another to choose between socialism or communism or capitalism, all of which were perfect and God-given. Millions were killed in the process, wealth was destroyed, whole populations were enslaved, all because a minority was convinced of the superiority of the ideologies they believed in and the ultimate heaven for the people which they were going to create.

When they could not conquer they subverted the people by spreading their ideology. Even as the capitalists ruled their colonies with an iron hand, the communists and the socialists promoted the supremacy of the state and its need to own all the means of production in order to spread the wealth of the nation. And many of us were convinced. In the early years of our independence, we nationalised everything, frequently seizing the properties and enterprises of the rich. Then we messed up everything with our inexperience and our wealth was destroyed. Far from becoming rich egalitarian states, we became poor and indebted to foreign agencies and banks. Soon we were working merely to service these loans.

In the meantime, the communists and the socialists of Europe were having second thoughts. After 70 years they finally decided their socialism and communism did not deliver the promises that they had made. Having convinced themselves that these ideologies were wrong they abandoned them. And the poor Asian and African countries which had been converted to socialism and communism were left stranded with massive poverty, huge debts and governments which were not only inefficient but oppressive as well.

While the communists and the socialists were gaining ground in Europe, the capitalists were making judicious adjustments to survive. They curbed their greed and put on a friendlier face. They accommodated their workers and allowed them to unionise, to strike and to form political parties. They increased the pay packets and social benefits. They renamed capitalism, 'market economics'. And so they not only survived but prospered as well.

The collapse of the communist bloc deprived the poor countries of the option to defect to the other side. Now there is only capitalism. The need for a friendly face for capitalism is no longer there. And so capitalism, baleful, unmitigated capitalism, is free to do what it likes.

But their countries have become too small for the capitalists and the huge capital they had amassed or invented. They need a bigger arena. They need the world for the maximum deployment of their capital. Borders which divide countries are barriers to their acquisitiveness and unlimited greed.

And so borders must be done away with. Why should there be borders in a world of instant communication and high-speed travel? There must be just one world for capital to operate in. Capital must be free to go anywhere regardless of borders.

Again the justification for this convinced them. Capital would enrich the poor countries through investments and financial skills. But best of all, capital would enable the best goods and services to be universally available at the lowest cost. The efficiency of the developed world would flow into the developing world, to create a better and richer society.

The developed ethnic European countries were convinced that they were actually doing the developing Asian and African countries a favour. It was the White Man's Burden all over again, only this time there were no gunboats. Money does a better job.

Malaysia and the countries of East Asia had developed fast after gaining independence. Instead of accepting wholesale the system and the ideologies of the West, we had devised our own system and maintained what we consider our Asian values. We embraced democracy, but not the liberal democracy of the West. We are relatively open.

We may not have the cleanest or the most incorruptible governments in the world, but we do care for our people and our country enough to work hard to develop and to progress, to industrialise and to build prosperous economies. In less than half a century we had converted our agrarian nations of poor peasants into fairly sophisticated industrialised economies. Our people were reasonably well-off, were employed and our poverty was reduced to a bare minimum. We believed that we could eventually join the privileged group of developed countries.

Then suddenly came disaster, not due to any natural catastrophe, not due to our doing something different, not revolution or civil war or invasion by our neighbours. The disaster that came was in the simple form of currency devaluation against the US dollar. The result was to impoverish us. Malaysia had a per-capita income of US$5,000 before. A devaluation of 70 per cent reduced the per-capita income to US$1,500. The per capita and the GDP of some other Asian countries are even worse.

But the currency is not the only target for attacks. The share markets were also attacked. Share prices tumbled, in some cases by 90 per cent, rendering companies incapable of paying debts or operating normally. Profits were greatly reduced or losses sustained.

The governments which depended on corporate taxes to finance administration and development are finding themselves bereft of funds. Social and political unrest explode and governments either become ineffective or are overthrown.

We are told that all these things are happening because our governments are corrupt and our countries are badly managed. Considering that we have been able to develop and prosper our countries remarkably well, this accusation seems strange. If we were badly managed, surely we would not have prospered, surely we would have suffered devaluation long ago.

But the Western media insisted again and again that the economic turmoil we are experiencing is of our own doing. We are told it is no good blaming others. Our governments are to be blamed for we are not transparent, we practise crony-capitalism and nepotism. Now market forces have come to discipline us, to teach us how to manage our countries properly.

Who are the market forces? Certainly they are not the locals. These market forces are foreign, located in some countries where they cannot be seen. Taking advantage of their ability to breach borders with their capital, they are able to devalue currencies at will. And when our currencies are devalued, we will suffer. But how else can you discipline people if you don't make them suffer?

Today, tens of millions of workers have lost their jobs, thousands of companies have been made bankrupt, banks and finance companies have closed down, taking along with them the deposits of their clients. Today, millions of people are without food and medicine. Today, governments are unable to function, much less to help the suffering masses. Today, shops are looted, people are raped and killed. And all these things and more are happening because our governments have to be disciplined, to be forced to become transparent, to remove obstruction to the free flow of foreign capital, to the purchase and control by foreigners of national banks and businesses.

We are told that this is how the globalised world functions. The media tells us that this turmoil, all this impoverisation of our people and our countries, is good for us because they will help us to get good government, help us attract foreign investments.

While the market forces were disciplining us, they were making billions of dollars for themselves. Apparently the market forces have to be well-paid for disciplining governments.

I am sorry, but we still think it is a gross injustice. We believe it is inhuman to impoverish millions of people in order that capital should flow freely. We think it is unjust to destroy the prosperity of countries in order to realise a globalised, borderless world. We believe there must be a better way to discipline governments, a way which does not cause misery for innocent people.

We believe in globalisation. Yes, we want the prosperity that a free flow of capital can bring. But what we are experiencing is not prosperity but massive impoverishment. Since this is not what we expect, since this is not what is good for us, can we not ask that there be some rules and regulations governing the flow of capital?

But we are told currency trading is special. It cannot be regulated or made transparent. It cannot be taxed. It is the essence of a free market.

The ethnic Europeans, having given up communism and socialism, have now embraced capitalism wholeheartedly. Nothing must stand in the way of capitalism. Globalisation, deregulation, liberalisation, borderless world—these are the fundamentals of the new theology. The high priests are the people with capital, unlimited capital. Their handmaidens are the great writers, journalists and economists, the media practitioners who propagate the religion with fervour. And like all religious fanatics they tolerate no recalcitrance.

It is a pity, all these. It is a pity because the world is indeed getting smaller and we are all getting closer to one other. National boundaries are indeed anachronistic because we can see and hear each other across borders and across vast spaces. Nothing happens in one part of the world that does not affect other parts, affects immediately sometimes, affects profoundly. We can no longer isolate ourselves. No man, no nation, is an island. The world is our country, the nation to which we belong. Globalisation is therefore the right way, the inevitable consequence of information technology.

But like everything else, globalisation needs to be carefully managed if it is to benefit us. It is a means to an end, not an end in itself. Globalisation must result in a better life for everyone in this world. If it does not, then we have to reexamine it, not to do away with it, but to eliminate whatever is harmful and promote that which is good.

Remember that the Western ideologies have been wrong so many times before. They could be wrong again. They could be wrong about globalisation, at least about their interpretation or concept of globalisation.

We must globalise, but we must do so carefully and slowly. We must recognise that the countries whose borders we are going to dismantle are not all of the same strength or level of development. They need to be protected from the predators, at least for some time. Surely the rich and the powerful can wait.

Malaysia, for example, cannot have an automobile industry if it has no borders. The industry is protected because there is no way we can go into it if foreign cars are allowed in tax-free or with very low import duty. By taxing imports at a fairly high rate, locally manufactured cars can compete in the local market. As a result of that, the industry became viable. And in the meantime, the industry spun off numerous engineering industries which contributed to the industrialisation of the country.

Clearly, for Malaysia, industrialisation has been made possible because we erect barriers at our borders. Our people have to pay for this with higher prices. But the end result is an industrialised and more prosperous country. Foreign countries also benefited for we became a good market for their goods. We could import billions of dollars worth of goods and services.

It is now argued by the developed countries that Malaysia would benefit if we allow for unrestricted and tax-free imports of low-cost goods from the highly efficient industries of the developed countries. We would be able to buy the best products at the lowest price.

But if we do not industrialise we will not develop. Our people will remain unemployed and poor. Even if the imported products are of good quality and cheap we will not be able to afford them.

Yes, we should globalise but countries must be allowed to open up in their own time, when they are ready. We should also not confine borderlessness to capital only. People too should be able to cross borders freely.

The rich countries, particularly those with vast uncultivated land, should allow for the migration of people from poor countries. Just as the financial capital of the rich will benefit poor countries, the hardworking peoples of the poor countries can benefit the rich countries.

Globalisation is a great idea whose time has come. But it must be interpreted correctly if it is ever going to bring about a better life for everyone in this world. Presently we are not too convinced that it is going to be good for us in the developing countries. We have seen how the free flow of capital has damaged our economies and we fear that globalisation may turn out to be like socialism or communism, ideas which were touted for a time and were then discarded as wrong. Globalisation might one day go the way of imperialism, communism and socialism. But we are willing to give it a try, though at our own pace. We would like the proponents of globalisation to remember that it may be harmful. We would like them to accept the need for consulting us and for our complaints and suggestions to be heard and when legitimate be accepted.

Globalisation may yet be the route to equitability for the peoples and nations of a borderless world. I would therefore like to pledge my support for a globalisation that is concerned not just with the means but also the ends. Let us form smart partnerships. Let us have good governance. But let us not forget that our quest is for the well-being of our people. The best ideology, system or philosophy means nothing if the result does not bring about justice, fair play and prosperity for all.

18

The Future of Asia in a Globalised and Deregulated World

"In the globalised deregulated world the future of Asia will be so closely intertwined and interlinked with that of the rest of the world that it cannot be distinguished from the world's future."

JUST a year ago it was so easy to talk about the future of Asia. One needs only to trot out figures regarding growth, the areas of growth, the relative growth rates of the different countries of Asia, when the countries would qualify to join the OECD

A speech delivered at the Nihon Keizai Shimbun International Conference in Tokyo, Japan, on June 4, 1998

countries and when they will graduate and become developed countries.

Today, predicting the future of Asia is more difficult because in the space of a few months, the Asian countries in the East have shown that they have clay feet, that under pressure they can all collapse and become beggars, appealing for aid from international institutions, promising to discard their evil ways, which had led to high growth and low inflation. If they fail to do this, worse still if they dare to argue that their economic turmoil is not caused by them and them alone, then their economies would suffer a worse degree of economic recession. This is because such recalcitrance will cause a greater loss of confidence amongst the market forces and when their confidence is lost, then the economies of the recalcitrants must suffer.

This is perhaps strange in a world which talks incessantly about the freedom of speech, about human rights. It is even more strange that millions of people being made jobless and destitute does not arouse the sympathy of the exponents of human rights. Their response this time is simply to point at the governments of these countries and accuse them of a variety of social crimes. That for 40 years these same governments had developed their countries and created millions of jobs for their people was dismissed as the ill-gotten gains of their corruption.

Now that they have been made aware that their ways and past performance were bad and unacceptable and that they had led to a loss of confidence on the part of market forces, they are expected to carry out reforms quickly.

The reforms are spelt out by international agencies and the media and their implementation is crucial for the return of confidence and the rehabilitation of the economy. Backing these institutions are the major economic powers who had contributed to the funds for the rescue of these countries. The G7, at its recent meeting in Birmingham, England, clearly express their expectation that the governments of the distressed economies of East Asia would heed the IMF's directives if they want their countries' economies to be restored.

What are these directives that are expected to restore the Asian economies to their former levels of prosperity?

The first directive is to increase interest rates. Then there should be a credit squeeze. There should also be an increase in taxes.

In addition, all subsidies and monopolies must be withdrawn and the government should not control exports.

Finally, the countries receiving IMF aid must open up their economies so that foreign companies could operate without any restrictions on ownership or areas of economic activity.

Even when a country's economy is strong and doing well, these directives are likely to slow down economic growth, especially the part contributed by locals. But these countries are under stress economically as their currencies have been devalued by 50 per cent to 600 per cent. Furthermore, the share prices have collapsed due to massive withdrawal of capital by foreign investors. Effectively this devaluation of the currency and the share prices would result in the collapse of practically all the business. Foreign loans would require more local currency, between 50 per cent and 400 per cent more, in order to repay. Local bank loans based on the share prices would also require more money as the value of the shares as collaterals fall below the amount of loan taken. The economic turmoil into which the country had plunged makes it difficult to do business and make profits. But if the loans are to be paid the profits must be extraordinary.

But when the interest rate is increased and credit is pulled back, the task of making additional profit is made quite impossible. Eventually the banks must take action to foreclose. Between the currency and share devaluation and the interest rate increase and credit squeeze most of the nations' companies will go bankrupt.

The bankruptcies of so many companies must affect the banks as well as the government. Banks will accumulate non-performing loans while losing valuable clients and there will be no new clients due to the recession. Governments of countries which depend on corporate taxes to fill their coffers will suffer gross reduction in revenue and the capacity to sustain operational and development expenditures.

There is, of course, one possible avenue for escape and resuscitating the economy. The devaluation of the currency and the fall in share prices render the local companies and banks attractive for takeovers by foreign companies. Since one of the conditions for aid is to open the country to unrestricted foreign investments, it would be easy and extremely cheap for foreign companies to acquire the distressed local companies, including huge utilities such as telecommunications and power. It is also possible for foreign investors to set up 100-per cent foreign-owned banks, utility companies, land and sea transport, etc.

Since the foreign companies moving in are all sound companies with good capital backing, market confidence would be regained, resulting in the appreciation of the currency as well as recovery of the stock market.

In other words, the takeover of the economy by foreign companies would result in economic recovery.

In a globalised borderless world people should not mind their economies being controlled by foreigners as long as they can get the services of the most efficient and financially powerful companies of the world. Banks and corporations should allow themselves to be absorbed by the big foreign banks and corporations. People should be happy to work for foreign companies since they are likely to receive better pay.

Unfortunately, some countries are resisting globalisation and are trying to overcome the problems caused by currency devaluations and the dive in share prices on their own. They are trying to help their banks and companies by restructuring and making credit available. This is considered as carrying out bailouts and this will cause a loss of confidence on the part of market forces. The result will be further devaluation of the currency and falls in share prices. Eventually these countries must give in and accept the inevitable.

Before we can guess what the future is going to be like, we have to look at the past and the present, including the immediate present which is more likely to develop and become a part of the future.

In the heyday of blatant capitalism, i.e. in the second half of the 19th century and the beginning of the 20th century, exploitation of poor workers was considered as a matter of right. The vote was expected to be confined to property owners and workers should consider themselves lucky if they could find jobs with low pay. The rich took everything for themselves.

Marx argued that the wealth produced was the result of the labour of the working class. It was an injustice to deny them the full benefits of their labour. In fact, he felt that the workers should own the means of production. Thus began the socialist and communist revolutions which resulted in the loss of property and millions of lives. In many countries the viciousness of the revolution was unprecedented, with all the capitalists being massacred and their property confiscated. Dictatorships of the proletariat, the working classes, were established with all the means of production taken over by the communist state. The socialist were less violent but they too deprived the capitalists of their wealth and pushed for greater rights and privileges for the working classes.

Awakening to the danger of workers' revolutions and the violent takeover of governments, Western capitalists decided to display a friendlier face to their workers. The rights of the workers to form unions, to have higher wages and bonuses, to shorter working hours and holidays, to good housing and medical treatment were recognised and granted. Oppressive and unhygienic work conditions were eliminated. In some countries the workers even sit on the management boards of companies. Many socialistic practices were adopted to placate the workers.

The term capitalism was gradually displaced by the free market. Ownership of companies was spread to the middle class and working class through public limited companies. Altogether businesses became more democratic. The ugly capitalist image of private corporations was replaced by a much friendlier professionally managed public listed companies.

The new capitalists successfully contributed to the growth of their countries' economies. In the war against the national socialists, the capitalists actually collaborated with the communists in order to defeat the dictatorships of the fascists. Through a series of astute capital management, including a stable exchange-rate system crafted by economists at Bretton Woods, the Western neo-capitalists or free marketeers were able to rebuild their economies through a combination of capitalist and socialist approaches. But the underlying greed of the capitalist never really disappeared.

The communists, on the other hand, did not do so well economically. The idea that with everyone receiving the same pay and subsidies they would work just as hard and be equally happy did not prove right. Productivity and wealth decreased and the working classes no more appreciate their own dictatorship as they would capitalist dictatorship.

Eventually, the communist system collapsed. While they were around they provided a counter-balance to the capitalists of the West and made available the option to defect to the small countries. Without them the capitalists felt free to do as they pleased and small countries had no choice but to accept the domination of the big and the powerful.

Accordingly, the capitalist no longer feel the need to show a friendlier face. With the ease of communication their field has become enlarged. Instead of just aiming for acquisition of the national wealth they can now go for the wealth of the world. But to do this, certain concepts and values that they had preached in the past had to be reversed.

The concept of the nation-states and their independence had to be debunked. Non-interference in the internal affairs of nations must give way to the right of the powerful nations to intervene in order to ensure that the right things are done. Even democracy has to be sacrificed in favour of market forces in determining policies and government leadership.

Former US President Jimmy Carter was the first to claim the right to intervene in any country where human rights are alleged to have been violated. This was followed by the attempt to use the GATT and the WTO to link trade with human-rights records, workers' rights (specifically low wages in countries competing with the developed countries), the environment, etc.

The targets of these sudden concern for the people's well-being seem to be those developing countries which clawed their way into becoming industrialised nations producing goods which compete successfully with those of developed countries. The results of linking trade with human rights, etc would be to make the cost of production of these countries increase so much that they would not be able to compete at all or they may not be able to export their products at all. It is not unreasonable to assume that this concern for the well-being of the peoples of these countries was more because of the desire to make their goods less competitive against the goods of the developed countries.

Ugly capitalism seems to be at the back of this humanitarian concern. It is not humane at all as the consequence of this demand is to make the peoples of these countries poorer—not richer. Obviously they stand to lose the market if they comply and to be shut out of the market if they don't.

The developing countries saw through this scheme and opposed it in the GATT and the subsequent WTO. The opposition was muted, however, as the poorest countries with probably even worse records of human-rights violation were not involved as they were not producing anything to compete with the goods of the developed countries. Besides, most of these countries are under obligation to the developed countries from whom they had obtained aid or loans.

Nevertheless, the attempt to eliminate competition by low-cost countries failed.

The advent of the Information Age and instant communication brought forth the idea of the world without borders, a world in which not only information but capital, goods and people could move freely and exploit business potential without regard for citizenship or loyalties.

The exploitation of business opportunities by the people with the capital and the know-how in most countries has always been restricted by national laws which favour the citizens of a country. But because the citizens are poor and do not have the necessary know-how these opportunities have not been fully exploited. If the opportunities and potentials are to bring the maximum benefit to the people, then laws and regulation which favour locals must be done away with. In other words, there should be massive deregulation.

With such deregulation there would be, businesswise, no more borders to hinder the activities of those with the capital and the know-how from the most advanced and richest countries. The whole world would be just one country, open to everyone who knows and can exploit the business potential to the maximum. Thus as a corollary to deregulation there should be globalisation.

The developing countries were told that deregulation and globalisation would be good for their people. Without these they would forever be saddled with incompetent and poorly capitalised local businesspeople, usually the cronies of the leaders, who would provide inferior goods and services at exorbitant prices.

Paralleled with the propaganda on deregulation and globalisation came exposures of the misdeeds, the corruption and the cronyism of the leaders of countries which incidently had managed to industrialise themselves and produce goods to compete with those from industrialised countries. Inundated with these propaganda material from the capitalist-controlled world press, the peoples of these countries soon turned against their governments. They joined the chorus not only to demand the overthrow of their governments but to open up their countries to foreign exploitation.

Obviously only the biggest corporations can dominate the world. In preparation for this global domination the big corporations and banks in certain countries are already taking steps through mergers and acquisitions to grow even bigger. It is felt that in any one field of business there needs to be only a few giant corporations—three or four for the whole world would be enough. The small national corporations must allow themselves to be acquired or to perish in the one-sided competition.

Unfortunately, for the powerful advocates of globalism and deregulation, the most highly developed of the developing countries did not take too kindly to these ideas of deregulation and globalisation. They did not reject them completely but begged to be given time to strengthen their companies and banks. Their delaying tactics merely made the giant countries and their corporations impatient. Somehow they must be forced to speed up.

It is to the credit of the powerful economies of the West and their giant corporations that they did not conspire. But the opportunity was thrown into their laps when the currency traders attacked and devalued the currencies of all those developing countries which were delaying globalisation. The short-term investors in the share markets of the countries attacked by the currency trader then pulled out their capital causing a drastic fall in the share prices and aggravating the economic situation.

Faced with this unprecedented financial crisis in which the national wealth was at least halved the governments of these developing countries had to ask for the help of the International Monetary Fund (IMF). As the IMF believed that recovery could only be brought about by foreign companies taking over partially or completely the local companies distressed by the falls in the currency and shares, one of the conditions insisted upon by the Fund was the removal of the restrictions on ownership of local banks and companies by foreign investors. As a result of the countries accepting this condition foreign companies could acquire all the big and profitable companies or hold controlling interest in them. These foreign companies would be giants which operate globally. Their funds would be huge and they would dominate the world.

There was a time when big American companies own huge banana plantations in some of the poor Latin American republics. The revenue of the governments of these republics came almost exclusively from the banana plantation companies. If the companies fail the republics would be in grave trouble. It was in the interest of these republics to accede to the demands of the companies, including political adjustments. It is just possible that the giant corporations which operate in the countries which have been persuaded to open up will have the same influence over the governments.

It has been pointed out that currency traders can devalue any nation's currency at will. Currency trading is done not by hedge funds alone, but also by the big banks. One of these banks is capitalised at over US$600 billion. It is believable that between these banks and the currency traders they have almost US$30 trillion.

They do not work in concert, of course. Nor do they enter into a conspiracy. But they do exhibit herd-like behaviour. Thus, when one of the more important members swing in one direction, the other will follow. The effect is not unlike acting in concert.

The devaluation of the currencies of East Asia is said to be due to corrupt crony-capitalism. They will deny that their corruption is the cause of their currencies' devaluation even as the currency traders deny that they have anything to do with the devaluation. But whoever may be guilty the fact is that the currencies have been devalued massively, in one instance by 600 per cent. We can assume that the currencies are intelligent and they devalue themselves when the governments which issue them misbehave.

What is a fact, however, is that the countries whose currencies have been devalued suffer economically, socially and politically. If because of their profligate ways they were unable to pay their foreign debts, after devaluation they become even less able to pay their debts. This will awaken them to their poor skills in managing their companies and they would be more willing to accept the capital, services and control by foreign companies.

The net result of the globalised deregulated world would be the emergence of huge corporations and banks with branches in every country in the world. Their numbers would not be too big as all the small companies and banks would have been acquired or absorbed in one way or another.

In the old capitalism, the rich controlled the wealth in one or two countries and exploited the poor workers in these countries only. Their markets were the empires that they had acquired. These were captive markets, which not only bought all the manufactured products at whatever price that was fixed, but also supplied all the raw materials at prices which were fixed by the rich industrialists in the metropolitan countries.

This arrangement was neat. Unfortunately, in the postwar years the empires had to be dismantled. Preoccupation with the Cold War and the need to retain the allegiance of the newly independent countries kept the capitalists at bay. But once the challenge posed by the communist bloc was overcome the capitalists were let loose.

Today, it is not the exploitation of local labour that is the focus of the new capitalists. It is the exploitation of the poor countries worldwide that promises unlimited gains. Hence the push for deregulation and globalisation.

These capitalists do not talk of millions of dollars of profits. They talk of billions of dollars. They cannot wait to do ordinary businesses involving time-consuming research, manufacturing and exporting. They want to make their billions overnight. And currency trading provides them with these mind-boggling profits.

With trillions at their disposal they have become a force that no government of developing countries can go against. Control of the media enables them to shape public opinion, censor criticism and generally promote the legitimacy and the wholesomeness of their concept of the new world order. If they say globalism is good then the whole apparatus will say so and no one will be allowed to say otherwise.

I have briefly described the past and the present. So what is going to be the future, the future of Asia. Actually there is not going to be much of a future for Asia, at least a future that is distinctly Asian. In the globalised deregulated world the future of Asia will be so closely intertwined and interlinked with that of the rest of the world that it cannot be distinguished from the world's future.

Asian countries will prosper again but not as Asian countries. Their economies would be dominated and run by the huge foreign corporations, practically all owned and managed by non-Asians. Southeast Asia will provide a base for the production of low-cost products to compete with those of certain large Asian economies which refuse to be controlled. In the end these countries too will give in.

Governments will submit because they know they are up against forces which they cannot defeat. But the people will show their resentment against those outsiders who will lord it over them once again. Bitter over the takeover of their national corporations, they will show their feelings in many ways. Sooner rather than later they will think of regaining control over their economies. They will regard this as a new war of liberation. Even if they want to avoid violence, violence must come as the new capitalists disregard the signs. There will be no war of independence, of course. But there will be a kind of guerrilla war which will not be good for anyone.

Maybe this will not be the future of Asia. Maybe Asia will extricate itself from the present situation intact. Maybe the healthy economic competition between Asia, Europe and America will be restored. But the new capitalists would not want to miss the opportunity to dominate the world and make lots of money in the process. Only if their own countries restrain them will the future of the world of which Asia is a part be peaceful and prosperous.

19

The Challenge of Globalisation

"With all these threats and obstructive actions we must now face the challenge of globalisation. Are we in a state to face this challenge? Quite obviously not. But no one is going to wait for us to get ready for the challenge. So whether we like it or not we have to face the challenge."

SMART partnerships clearly can take place between many entities. Apart from government and the private sector, and nations in a region there can be smart partnerships between individuals, between companies, between twin cities and a host of others.

A speech delivered at the 1st Southern Africa International Dialogue (SAID) in Kasane, Botswana, on May 5, 1997

I believe the South African Development Cooperation (SADC) too will evolve into a smart partnership and this inaugural South African International Dialogue (SAID) 1997 will definitely accelerate the process. I am most happy to note that SAID 1997 is the second International Dialogue to take off after the Langkawi International Dialogue launched in 1995. The first one ᴖ was the Barbados International Dialogue for Small Nation-States (BID 1996) last year. Other regions may follow suit. When such a time comes, it will usher in a new understanding between regions and groupings which may contribute to an era of global peace and prosperity, a Commonwealth of the world where wealth would truly be common.

However, smart partnership is just one element in the formula for success. Systems and formulae by themselves cannot guarantee success. This is because other elements play a role and can affect the success or otherwise of a formula or system. And so smart partnership depends also on the environment, not the trees and forests but the political and economic environment within the country and without, the culture and the value system of the people, and a lot of other minor elements.

Asean and SADC share many common features, one of which is that many of the member states in these two organisations were former colonies of countries from the Imperial North. Malaysia was lucky that the transition from a British colony to an independent nation was a peaceful one. Many others were not so lucky and they had to endure the traumas of bloodshed and civil strife before they could achieve independence from their colonial masters. And this invariably has a deleterious effect on their subsequent development.

But can we developing countries be truly independent? Undoubtedly, direct occupation and political control has ended but this has been replaced by much more insidious forms of colonisation. Indeed, many of us have found that we are more dependent than when we were colonies. Our politics, economy, social and behavioural systems are all still under the control, directly or indirectly, of the old colonial masters and the great powers. And this constitute the environment in which we have to manage ourselves. Our struggle for independence is far from over.

As we all know the moment the European nations realised that they were all going to lose their empires, they decided to come together in order to continue their grip on international affairs. Today, the European Union is a powerful force which tries to impose its will on the rest of the world. For a time they were preoccupied with the East-West confrontation. But now that is over and a much more united Europe, which includes the Eastern states and Russia, will confront the rest of the world.

Their approach will be more subtle. Colonisation is over, but now comes globalisation. The borders which define countries will be erased and economic competition on a so-called level playing field must reign supreme. Globalisation and level playing fields have become the catchwords of a new religion and as we know, you do not challenge religious faith no matter how obviously wrong they are. You merely accept it.

Is it coincidental that globalisation seems to favour the rich and the powerful? We cannot protect our fledgling industries behind our borders anymore. They must compete with the giants of the world. Imagine the Malaysian car competing against cars produced by the millions by General Motors or Volkswagen or Daimler-Benz or Toyota. Malaysia has to pay a high price for a small part of the technology and buy a whole lot of overpriced components. Can Malaysia's cost of production, despite low labour cost be as low as the millions of cars coming from the robotised and automated assembly lines of the rich? And yet we are told to open up the market. Our GSP is about to be withdrawn. And all these on the alter of globalisation, transparency, borderlessness, fair wages and level playing fields.

Malaysia used to be the biggest producer of tin and rubber in the world. It became rich, or at least people like Guthrie, Boustead, Sime, and many others became rich, because of these two commodities. About the time we became independent synthetic rubber was developed, and instead of tin cans, food and other products are packed in plastic, aluminium, paper and glass containers. The bottom was knocked off our only foreign exchange earners. Our commodities lost their earning capacity and prices could not keep up with the ever-increasing prices of manufactured goods we have to import, some of which are made from our own raw materials. Open and free competition is great but every time we open and we compete, we lose out. How is that? Should the South confine itself to the real playing field, to soccer and cricket fields, where we stand a chance of winning and leave the economic playing fields to our betters? I think we should, but now our best players will be bought by the rich so they may get all the gold for themselves on the real playing fields too.

I am not saying this out of bitterness. Malaysia has done reasonably well. Asean has done reasonably well. But what I have mentioned are facts, hard facts, which will have a bearing on the future of all developing countries.

In the WTO, who comes up with new catchphrases such as globalisation, the environment, child labour, workers rights, borderless world, level playing fields, etc? It is invariably the economically powerful nations of the North. And for some reason or other, all the solutions to these issues or problems will result in economic gains for the rich.

How our workers sweated and toiled during the colonial period was not an issue before, but it is an issue now. Millions of acres of prime forests in Malaysia were cut down and burnt in order to grow rubber and mine for tin in the colonial days, and nobody cared. Today, environmentalists demonstrate against us and boycott our timber because we build a dam to provide cheap electricity for our people.

I appreciate the genuine concern and the cooperation on the part of many from the developed countries about developing the poor countries. But I would like to warn developing countries here and elsewhere that there will always be things that the developed will do which will not benefit us. We will face many obstacles, one of the worst is the corruption of our governments with aid in order that we will not speak freely about what is being done against us. Very frequently developing countries are forced to support the stand of developed countries or face loss of aid or some material support. Time and again, developing countries are divided and splintered when debating issues such as market access or GSP rights, as a result of which they all lose out.

Aid is welcome but aid with strings attached often negate the help extended. In the early years of the IMF, developing countries were persuaded to borrow money for development. This they did with a great deal of hope. But today most developing countries which borrowed from the World Bank are deeply in debt. In some cases fully 80 per cent of their meagre foreign exchange earnings go towards paying debts, leaving them totally unable even to pay the salaries of government employees. And as is customary with banks, when you most need loans, that is when they rate you as not creditworthy and refuse to lend to you. The IMF is no different. Today, the net flow has been reversed and the World Bank receives more in loan payments than the loans they give out. The World Bank is profitable for the shareholders who are almost all rich developed countries.

But having lent money to the poor countries, the World Bank insists on directing the management of the economy of these countries.

The advice they give is calculated to benefit the repayment of loans they had given out. The political effects of their directives do not bother them. Frequently countries are destabilised and governments overthrown due to following the advice of the World Bank.

Now, of course, the obsession is with liberal democracy and the multiparty system. I am all for democracy. Malaysia has many political parties and the opposition invariably win seats in Parliament and in the legislative councils of the states. Opposition parties have formed governments in several states and they still control one state. But the democratic system is not the easiest system to operate.

The present liberal democratic countries in the North have had over 200 years of experience. They became democratic slowly. Even today they are in the process of developing the system.

But the former colonies which gained independence in the post-World War II period had to go from autocratic government operated by the metropolitan countries to self-administered democracy, overnight literally. How do people who had never known democracy suddenly make this complex system work?

Many developing countries which adopted the one-party system failed because they had had no experience in government. Now they are being told to have a multiparty system, to have elections to choose a government. Many only understand the freedom that they are entitled to, not at all the responsibility, least of all the intricate workings of a multiparty democracy. And so they take to the streets to demonstrate, they have general strikes and generally they destabilise the nation in the belief that they are exercising democratic rights. In one former communist European country the people exercised their so-called democratic right by continuous street demonstrations. The government was rendered helpless. Armories were raided and guns seized by rioters. Law and order broke down completely. Innocent people, including children, were killed. Finally, foreign troops had to be called in to forcibly restore law and order in the country. And all these because people who had never known democracy suddenly had democratic freedom thrust upon them. Can we blame them if the whole thing went to their heads?

It is assumed that people will know what is good for them and in a democracy they have the right to determine for themselves what the government should be doing. But it is a fact that people can also be corrupted by the power they wield in a democracy. Their decisions are not always good for them. They are as likely to shoot themselves in the foot as anyone else in power.

People choose representatives and parties not because they are capable of forming good clean governments. They choose people because they hate the previous government for imposing necessary taxes or for collecting taxes. Good government is very often far from their minds. Instead, they may simply hate the government even though the government had brought prosperity to them. Then they may allow themselves to be instigated into bringing down a government to help achieve the narrow ambitions of politicians who are corrupt or intend to rape the nation of its spoils.

Mass movements in a democracy can be whipped into a frenzy by irresponsible politicians. Far too many multiparty democratic countries have been quite unable to have effective governments because no party has been able to gain a good majority. Post-election coalitions of weak parties which constantly bicker amongst themselves have proven to be worse than no government. The country suffers politically and economically. Poverty spreads, infrastructure and public utilities and services collapse. And people generally suffer. The nation becomes weak and is manipulated by powerful nations. Debts mount and eventually the country goes bankrupt.

All these things are actually happening. These are not hypothetical cases. They are happening not because democracy is a bad system. They are happening because people assume that systems can solve problems. Systems do not solve anything. People do. Democracy, or for that matter any form of government, can bring about development and a good life for the people if the people know how the system works and the limits of the system. The best political or government system requires discipline from the people in order to make them work. The value system and the political understanding of the people is important. They must not expect to get everything for themselves. They must accord power to the government, i.e. they must accept unpleasant decisions made by the government as for example imposing taxes and collecting them, limiting freedom, regulating a whole lot of things which may prevent untoward things from happening. Above all, they must allow the government to govern and not distract it by destabilising actions. If the country is to be democratic the government should be removed only through regular elections. And, of course, the government must never abuse its power.

A multiparty liberal democratic system is not something which everyone is familiar with, least of all a newly independent country which had been ruled autocratically by foreigners as a colony for decades or even centuries. To expect such a country and its people at the midnight lowering of the imperial flag to suddenly practise the most sophisticated form of liberal democratic government is insane. To expect a true and proper election even is too much.

We should go for democracy, of course. But we should be tolerant of the fumbling attempts, the failures and the mismanagements. The world must help in the training of government in the management of the economy. We should not expect the ultimate. We should not tolerate the dictators who emerge. But we should understand why they emerged. They emerge because we impose a system on people who do not understand or had no experience of working the system.

The old League of Nations used to set up trust territories. Unfortunately, the objective was to perpetuate colonisation. But the trusteeship could be used to provide a period of supervision which can be applied to certain countries which have no inkling of democracy. Countries like Rwanda, Burundi, Bosnia Herzegovina and a few others could benefit from the UN moving in early in order to oversee the transition from autocratic colonial rule to democracy and economic management. This way less damage would be done than waiting until hundreds of thousands are massacred, or the economy totally destroyed before the UN offers tepid help, or the World Bank begins to advise. Liberal democracy and the totally free market can do as much damage or even more damage than limited democracy and a less open market.

The moment the North lost their colonies in the South, they set up the European Economic Community (EEC) which today has become the European Union (EU), a very powerful economic entity capable of forcing its will on the South that they had raped before and impoverished through unfavourable terms of trade. But the North has not finished yet. They have formed the Group of Seven (G7) to totally dominate the world, to colonise it by other means.

For example, when Japan flooded the international market with their cheap yet high quality goods, the rest of the G7 pushed up the value of the yen in order to make the Japanese less competitive and to regain their markets. For the poor in this world, cheap Japanese goods enabled them to enjoy such luxuries as radios, televisions and pickup trucks, even motorcars. But the revaluation of the yen following the so-called Plaza Accord pushed up prices of Japanese goods out of the reach of the poor in poor countries.

But the Japanese had already invested for production in the lower-cost countries of Southeast Asia. A campaign was mounted in the International Labour Organisation (ILO) by trade unions of the North to push up labour costs in Southeast Asia to negate the competitive advantage these countries offer to the Japanese. Workers in these countries were urged to demand high wages and to destabilise the country through industrial actions so that foreign investors would shy away. The ultimate result of the sympathy of trade unions of the North for our workers is to push cost up, reduce direct foreign investments and reduce employment opportunities for the workers. This way the workers in the

North will not face unemployment, will continue to enjoy high wages, and a high standard of living.

I will not speak about the linking of non-trade issues with trade and the threat of sanctions because we all know that it is not because of concern for our environment or workers' rights, all of which in the end will stifle our economic development and impoverish our people. But I would like to mention about the effect of the yen revaluation on the yen loans to developing countries. Because the value of the yen has increased 2.5 times the rate of exchange with the Malaysian ringgit at the time we borrowed, our debts in Malaysian ringgit has also increased by 2.5 times. We now have to find 2.5 ringgit plus interest for every 100 yen we had borrowed when in fact 100 yen before the Plaza Accord was equal to only a ringgit. And all because the G7 wanted to solve their deficits in trade with Japan. Japan is not the one paying. We of the South, the recipients of the so-called cheap yen loans, are the ones who are paying.

The G7 is snooty. They will not condescend to talk with people outside their club except with Russia. We have asked to at least be allowed to have our views heard before they decide on matters affecting us but we have been totally ignored. They refuse to talk to the Chairman of the Non-Aligned Movement (NAM). And they refuse to talk to the G15 countries or their representatives. This is of course democratic. In their democracy of old, only landlords had the right to vote. The common man had none. In modern day liberal international democracy, only the rich can have a say, the poor shall remain voiceless. And these same people preach *ad nauseam* about democracy to us.

We live in an international jungle. There is no law and order in international relations. There is very little justice. The high and the mighty rules. The weak and the poor just have to lump it.

With all these threats and obstructive actions we must now face the challenge of globalisation. Are we in a position to confront this challenge? Quite obviously not. But no one is going to wait for us to get ready for the challenge. So, whether we like it or not, we have to face the challenge.

The only way that the weak can face any challenge is to present a united front, better still, to form a smart partnership. We are here today because I believe we are interested in smart partnerships. Nations can come together to form smart partnerships. Not only will we be able to present a united front but through smart partnerships we can actually strengthen each other. We are not without assets and experience. By exchanging our experience in economic management, we can learn to do what is right and avoid the mistakes that any one of us may have made. By sharing whatever little assets we have we can consolidate our strength.

Not only should the countries of Southern Africa come together but they should establish contact and cooperate with groupings such as Asean or the Indian Ocean Rim countries. The regional organisations too can form smart partnerships. When faced with damaging proposals from the developed North the regional organisations can take a common stand. This we did at the WTO meeting in Singapore. And we prevailed.

At home we should form smart partnerships between the government and the private sector and also with the trade unions. We must ensure good government dedicated to developing the country and enriching the people.

We must be democratic by being willing to use the ballot box to determine who forms the government.

And having elected the government we must allow it to govern for the duration of its term. Elected government is not always good, but bringing it down through demonstrations and industrial actions does more harm than good. Here members of regional groupings can help supervise to ensure elections are fair. Unless the crimes committed are serious, new governments should not take revenge on previous governments.

Political stability is absolutely essential for economic development, for fending off the predators from the developed North, and for maintaining the hard-won independence of our nation. We must realise that left to them, the North that is, globalisation will become another form of colonisation. We had fought hard for independence. We had shed blood for it. But we must know that globalisation, the breaking down of national borders, will result in the loss of independence. How can we be independent nations if we have no borders.

The North can gain much by recolonising. But we do have the ultimate weapon. People are more mobile now. They can go anywhere. In a borderless world we can go anywhere. If we are not allowed a good life in our countries, if we are going to be global citizens, then we should migrate North. We should migrate North in our millions, legally or illegally. Masses of Asians and Africans should inundate Europe and America. If there is any strength that we have, it is in the numbers. Three-fourths of the world is either black, brown, yellow or some combination of all these. We will make all nations in the world rainbow nations.

This is how we will ultimately challenge globalisation. I hope we don't have to resort to this. But we will if we are not allowed a piece of the action, a piece of the cake, if we are not allowed to prosper in a borderless world.

217

We can try to learn from those from the North who have been successful a very long time. But they have forgotten how they succeeded. And they have no patience for those who do not seem to know the obvious, who seem not to want to follow advice, who tumble and stumble and keep on making mistakes.

We should know that globalisation has come. The world will be borderless. All barriers will be taken down. Everyone is free to go anywhere, to trade anywhere, to invest anywhere, to do business anywhere. We from the South, from the developing countries, can now go and set up our banks and industries, our supermarket and hotel chains in the rich North even as the Northerners can come into our countries to set up banks and industries, business chains, etc. The problem is that we don't have the banks and the industries and the business chains to go North to benefit from the freedom of globalisation. We don't even have them in our own countries, how do we benefit from the right to go North? Even if we have, they are tiny. The field will be level but we are midgets in a world of giants. The giants will come and the giants will conquer.

I do not want to be too pessimistic. There is some hope. There is hope if we can work together, if we can form smart partnerships, if we can help each other, if we can devise ways of mutual help for the benefit of partners.

20

Globalisation and What It Means to Small Nations

"A globalised world is not going to be a very democratic world. A globalised world is going to belong to the powerful, dominant countries. They will impose their will on the rest. And the rest will be no better off than when they were colonies of the rich."

THERE HAS BEEN much talk of late about globalisation, a process or a state of affairs that holds much promise for the future of Planet Earth and not a little trepidation amongst the peoples of many countries for whom even nationhood has not delivered the things that they had expected. They are yet hardly

A speech delivered at the Inaugural Lecture of the Prime Minister of Malaysia' Fellowship Exchange Programme in Kuala Lumpur, Malaysia, on July 24, 1996

nations, and now they are asked to forget their nationhood, some only recently gained, and go for globalisation, something that they cannot yet comprehend but which they know would be too big for them to handle.

The developing nations of the world far outnumber the developed. Most of them were until recently colonised by the imperial powers, all of whom were developed and all from the wealthy West. They, the colonised, had not forgotten those colonial days not so very long ago. They cannot forget that for centuries they had had colonial masters. Some were fair and proper, but most were overbearing and oppressive. But without exception they made it clear that they were the masters and the inhabitants of the colonial territories were subject people.

Admittedly most of these colonial territories did not exist as states prior to their colonialisation. They were just vast tracts of land, without defined territories and boundaries and thus sovereignty and government. The inhabitants largely had no concept of nation-states; rather they were divided into tribes, which moved freely over whole continents sometimes, sharing the territory with numerous other tribes. Their loyalties were tribal and not territorial.

It was the colonial powers who delineated the colonial territories and created well-defined states, disregarding completely tribal claims. The boundaries were straight lines drawn on maps without any regard for local lores or rights. And so the independent states which emerged from these delineations were peopled by mixtures of tribes and races with no common culture, history or origins. Thus two independent states next to each other may have the same cocktail of races and yet be totally unrelated legally or politically. That these tribes and races never really accepted the dividing lines and boundaries was considered irrelevant. It suited the tidy minds of the imperialists to divide and separate them and to regard them as different entities and administrative units, and so they must accept the boundaries as *fait accompli.*

When decolonisation took place after World War II the independent nations which emerged were totally artificial. The inhabitants of different races and tribes had got along with each other during the colonial period, but this was not by choice. The colonial masters imposed from above a semblance of unity. Traditional tribal enemies had to live with each other at peace or face the wrath of the authoritarian colonial government adept at playing them against each other or using one race to impose the rule of the colonial masters on the other and on the rest.

The artificial peace and harmony of the colonial territories were taken as real. Superficially together against the colonial masters, the different races seemed united enough to be the citizens of the newly-independent nations. But deep under the old animosities and enmities burnt.

Still these territories were aware of the artificiality of their boundaries and the entities they formed. The sophisticated amongst them, the educated leaders, appreciated the need to prevent a breakup of their new nation along tribal or racial lines. And so they determined very early on that the territories, ruled as a single entity by the colonial masters, should not be allowed to breakup to form separate states, whether the different races wish to or not. The regional organisations that these new countries formed affirmed and endorsed this 'no secession' principle.

Not all of these regional organisations subscribed to this 'no secession' principle. Some of these colonial entities did break up into separate states, while others broke up after independence. Only a few managed to stay whole despite the tribal and racial loyalties which tended to break them up.

But whether the ethnic, racial and tribal groups remained in the same entity or not, they had problems managing relations between them. The problem was compounded if the races were also unequally developed.

During the colonial period the only form of government these peoples and territories knew were authoritarian colonial rule complete with detention without trial and banishment to remote parts of the world. Nevertheless these authoritarian colonial powers and their metropolitan governments insisted that the newly-independent countries adopt democratic forms of government with which they had no experience.

It is doubtful that the newly-independent countries would be able to manage whatever the form of government they were to adopt. A local version of the authoritarian form of government with which they were familiar would probably result in abuses of power and tyrannies. But trying to rule their countries through democratically elected representatives was certainly not the easiest thing for them to do. Besides, the previous masters were not going to allow them to manage even if they seemed able to adopt the democratic system. They were consistently harassed and badgered for not being democratic enough. And if they have minorities then they would be constantly accused of oppressing these minorities irrespective of the problems created by them. Nothing that the independent government did was right in the eyes of the former colonial masters. The fact that they, the former colonial powers, had never practised democratic administration was regarded as purely historical and irrelevant. The new countries must be perfect democracies according to the definition of the former masters.

Faced with the multifarious problems of tribal and racial divisions, lack of experience in government and understanding of democracy and its workings, it is a miracle that any of these newly-independent former colonial territories survive at all, much less prosper. But clearly all have survived even though some have to be propped up. Some are able to avoid civil strife and breakups, though almost none have been able to resolve their problems. Only a few manage to prosper despite their past colonial problems, but these are constantly harassed and badgered for not becoming what their previous colonial masters wanted them to be.

The fact is that almost none of these former colonial territories are any better politically and economically than they were before they became independent. In many aspects they were still very much colonised. Direct political occupation has ceased but colonialisation in other forms remains. The struggle for independence is therefore far from over.

Even those non-European countries which had never been colonised are not free from political, economic and social diminution. They too are being told how to run their countries, how to behave socially, how to maintain an environment safe for the rest of the world.

Devastated by tribal and civil wars, their resources manipulated through a market system controlled in far away places, unskilled in government and economic management, these developing countries look set to remain developing economies forever. Some indeed have regressed and are likely to continue regressing. Debts piled up, accumulating until whatever revenue they collect merely goes towards paying off their loans. Whole countries have been made debt-slaves of the rich nations, working for their masters with no prospect of ever securing their release.

But still these countries cherish their independence, limited though it may be. It seems to them that anything would be better than a return to being colonies of others no matter how much better off they would be. And now these countries are faced with globalisation, a single world in which they know they will have little say, their voices drowned, and their interest ignored in the pursuit of global interest and objectives as defined by others.

What does globalisation hold in store for the developing countries? As interpreted by the developed countries globalisation means the break down of boundaries as barriers to economic exploitation. Every country rich or poor, developed or developing would have access to every other country. The poor countries would have access to the markets of the rich, unrestricted. In return, or rather by right the rich will have access to the markets of the poor.

This sounds absolutely fair. The playing field will be level, not tilted to favour anyone. It will be a borderless world. It will be just one world. The whole of Planet Earth will be as one nation, and everyone will be earthlings, not subjects of countries or nations. Only then will globalisation be achieved.

But if there is only one global entity, there cannot be nations. Certainly there cannot be independence of nations. The newly-independent nations will disappear together with the old nations, including the former imperial or colonial powers. Everyone would be equal, citizens of the globe. But will they be truly equal?

After thirty years or more of 'independence' the former colonies of the West have found out the emptiness of the independence they had won. They have found that they are even more dependent than when they were colonies. They have found that their politics, their economy, their social and behavioral systems are all under the control, directly or indirectly of the old colonial masters and the great powers.

In the bipolar world of the Cold War period they had at least the option to switch allegiance even though allegiance often amounted to acceptance of hegemony. In a unipolar world they have lost even the choice to submit. They have to submit to the successful superpower and its cohorts whether they like it or not.

With that experience it is silly to think that globalisation will mean more independence for them, or mean more equitability for them. Globalisation can only mean one thing—loss of the nominal independence they have with nothing to compensate.

The GATT negotiations which held so much promise have resulted in the World Trade Organisation (WTO). What is the difference between WTO and GATT? The only tangible difference is that whereas the bilateral and multilateral trade agreements under the GATT were not internationally binding unless the parties concerned agree to submit to arbitration, the decisions of the WTO will be binding on all the members. Member countries will be punished by all the other members acting in unison. If for example the WTO decides to apply sanction then everyone would be bound to enforce the sanction.

Even now when the Western allies decided to apply sanction against Iraq, all other countries are forced to follow suit. If a decision is taken in the WTO there can be no exception.

Iraq, Iran and Libya are all labelled as rogue states. But will only those countries who are similarly guilty in the eyes of the West suffer such economic blockades? Will such blockades not be also applied to other 'crimes', e.g. human-rights violations, infringement of workers' rights, exploitation of child labour, environmental degradation, etc?

Already attempts are being made to link trade with these issues. It is clear that the developed countries wish to use the WTO to impose conditions on the developing countries which will result not in improving human rights or labour practices or greater care for the environment but in stunting their growth and consequently suffering for their people. Already the developed West have shown that they are not interested in these matters in themselves, but are interested in these only in those countries which pose a threat to the West. If these countries are absolutely poor and produce nothing that constitute a threat to the developed countries of the West, the plight of their people in terms of human rights or labour practices or the environment matter not at all. But if these countries are competing with the West in any way then their records are scrutinised and threats issued. The net effect is to prevent the development of these countries and their emergence as newly industrialising economies.

Globalisation would leave these developing countries totally exposed, vulnerable and unable to protect themselves. True globalisation may result in increasing foreign investments in these countries. But such investment will depend on the competitive advantages that these countries have. If investments like trade are linked to labour rights and wages, etc., then corrective measures taken by developing countries will remove their competitive advantage. Without these advantages, why should foreign investors invest in these countries?

On the other hand, if a fairly successful developing countries were to open their economies to all and sundry, the huge corporations in the developed countries will overwhelm the small companies in the developing countries. The huge banks, for example, will push aside the little banks of the developing countries. The big banks can afford to lose in a small country when they are making profits in their own country or in other developed countries. The local banks cannot afford such losses and will either shut down or be forced to merge and lose their identity. The same thing can happen to telecommunications companies, power companies, construction companies, etc.

The effect of economic globalisation would be the demise of the small companies based in the developing countries. Large international corporations originating in the developed countries will take over everything.

Perhaps international antitrust laws would be initiated and big corporations broken up. But experience has shown that the 'Baby Bells' soon grow and each becomes as big or bigger than their parent company. The same happened to the companies of the Japanese Zaibatsu.

The manufacturing, trading and telecommunications companies together with the banks will grow and merge, controlled and run by the huge core companies of the developed world. The little players from the small countries would be absorbed and would disappear. Their shareholders, big players when they were in the small companies, will wield insignificant authority in the huge conglomerates. And so will their CEOs and other executives, reduced to mere names on the payroll.

Nations differ not only because of their geographical and political compositions but more significantly because of their character and culture. Character and cul-

ture develop through the value systems of the society—
the exposure to these values and of course to the experience and surrounding sociopolitical environment
which members of a given society are exposed to.

Globalisation will result in all societies being exposed to the global culture. This is going to become
more universal because of the development of Information Technology (IT). The unfortunate thing is that the
IT industry, and all that will be disseminated through it,
will again be dominated by the big players—the huge
corporations owned by the developed countries. governments and the world may have the best of intentions
in terms of disseminating news and information but the
IT corporations may have other views.

Today sex and violence already dominate the
screens. Attempts to reduce this unwholesome fare
have met with little success. The appeal of thrill and sen-
suality are too great and too effective for the profit-ori-
ented companies to eschew these themes. With globalisation the effect of the 24-hour thousand channel TV
would be to standardise world culture as promoted by
the broadcasting giants of the world. They are not likely
to be conservative and responsible. They are going to
ensure that their companies outbid each other in terms
of profits.

Today's youth already wear the same uniforms—the
jeans. They keep their hair long and as untidy as possible. They only care for the pleasures of life. They have
little regard for traditional values, for age and the family
and institutions such as marriage and family. The problems of 'lepak' and 'bohsia', the careless disregard for
virtuous lifestyle—all these are related to the exposure
to foreign cultures.

The good aspects of foreign culture do not get an air-
ing. They are not interesting and entertaining. Besides,

good foreign cultural values are fast disappearing, victims of the same assaults by the media.

The present economic problems in the Western countries are the result of the changes in their culture. From being a disciplined and hardworking people they have become totally uncaring and unrestrained, demanding always less and less work, more leisure and more and more pay. Naturally their costs go up and they become uncompetitive. Faced with competition from the East and the new industrialised countries, they lose out. Their economy regress and they are unable to recover because their new culture has set in and cannot be changed back to the old values which had brought about their success in the first place.

Unwilling to give up the 'good life' as they imagine their way of life to be, they want to reduce competition by others through converting their competitors to their culture, their way of life. This they claim will result in their so-called level playing field, in which they stand more than an even chance to regain their superiority. And so again globalisation will result in the small nations remaining unable to catch up with the developed world.

But globalisation will not be confined to the economic and cultural field alone. The breaking down of borders will result in the powerful truly dominating the weak. Although the military forces can be a global force belonging to no particular nation, the fact remains that the financing and the command and control will be with the most experienced and the most skilled. And the poor nations are unlikely to dominate the military forces which will oversee the peaceful relations between countries and regions. We have already seen what happens to Bosnia-Herzegovina, where the fate of the Bosnians has been sidelined by the political interests of the European powers.

The law will be enforced by those countries which will be the most influential. Already we have seen how the president of a country had been arrested through a military operation by a powerful neighbour, taken back for trial and subsequently committed to prison in the neighbour's country. This involves the exercise of extraterritorial powers not provided for by any agreement. But there is nothing that anyone can do but accept the extraterritorial rights of the powerful. If the globalised world is dominated by a few countries then anyone can be arrested and tried by them. Of course, criminal leaders should be dealt with but what if the criminal leaders are from the powerful countries which control the global military force. Will the leaders be apprehended and brought to trial in a small country which has been the remote victim of the crimes of these leaders? It is most unlikely.

A globalised world is not going to be a very democratic world. A globalised world is going to belong to the powerful, dominant countries. They will impose their will on the rest. And the rest will be no better off than when they were colonies of the rich.

History would have turned a full circle within just two generations. Fifty years ago the process of decolonisation began and in a space of about twenty years was virtually completed. But even before all the colonies of the West have been liberated, indeed before any had become truly and fully independent, recolonisation has begun. And it is recolonisation by the same people.

They will of course refer to this as their burden, a responsibility which they have imposed on themselves. They will tell the world, the global community that they have no wish to impose themselves on anyone. But in a world where there is so much poverty, turmoil, riots and instability and frequent massacres, those responsible must not shirk their duty. They are only doing it for the good of everyone.

The year 1984 has come and gone. Big brother did not make his appearance. But that does not mean that Big Brother cannot appear after 1984. The technology for global scrutiny by Big Brother is available now. It remains for those in control to make use of this technology, and 1984 will become a reality.

This is what globalisation may be about. This is a gloomy prediction. It is pessimistic. It does not contain much hope for the weak and the poor. But unfortunately it is entirely possible. And it will be, unless the weak and the poor appreciates now this possibility and fight tooth and nail against it. There are ways of fighting the powerful. It will be a kind of guerrilla war. But it can succeed. And that war can only begin if there is understanding of what globalisation can mean.

Of course, globalisation may bring about Utopia, a paradise on earth, a world of plenty in which everyone can have everything. But nothing that has happened so far seems to justify this utopian dream. Just as the ending of the Cold War has brought about death and destruction to many people, globalisation may do exactly the same. Perhaps more.

Index

South African International
Dialogue, 182, 206
South-South Cooperation,
176

Toyota, 207

UNCTAD, *see* United
Nations Conference on
Trade and Development
United Nations Conference
on Trade and
Development, 97
United Nations General
Assembly, 175
United Nations Security
Council, 175
United Nations, 42, 175-176

United States, 35, 88, 90,
93-95

Volkswagen, 207
von Hayek, Friedrich, 45

World Bank, 22, 36, 41, 45,
51, 96, 120, 209-210, 213
World Trade Organisation,
10, 22, 32, 36, 45, 77, 89, 91,
94, 96-97, 104, 108-109,
115, 130, 135, 198, 208, 216,
225-226
World War I, 93
World War II, 20, 140, 175,
210, 221
WTO, *see* World Trade
Organisation

DR MAHATHIR MOHAMAD, one of the most durable and outspoken figures on the world political stage, has been prime minister of Malaysia since July 16, 1981. He first came to prominence in 1969 when he was expelled from the ruling party, UMNO, for writing a letter critical of the then prime minister, Tunku Abdul Rahman. Before being readmitted to UMNO in 1972, he wrote his famous, highly controversial work, *The Malay Dilemma*, which examined the economic backwardness of the Malays, and advocated state intervention to bring about their rehabilitation. The book was promptly banned in Malaysia. In *The Challenge* (1986), he explodes fallacies and exposes distortions concerning religion, education, democracy, communism, freedom and discipline, and the concerns of this world and the next. In *A New Deal for Asia* (1999), Dr Mahathir reflects on Malaysia's fight for independence and rails against those who blindly worship the free market.

As Malaysia's fourth prime minister, Dr Mahathir has played a pivotal role in the confident march of his people towards Vision 2020, his blueprint for Malaysia's advance towards fully developed status. Born on December 20, 1925, Dr Mahathir studied medicine in Singapore, where he met his future wife, Dr Siti Hasmah Mohd Ali. After working as a doctor in government service, he left to set up his own private medical practice in his hometown, Alor Setar. In 1974, he gave that up to concentrate on his political career. Dr Mahathir and his wife have seven children and ten grandchildren.

Islam and the Muslim Ummah

Mahathir Mohamad

One subject which is dear to Dr Mahathir Mohamad's heart and which he takes seriously is Islam and the Muslim *ummah* In this collection of speeches, he shares his thoughts on Islam, the Muslim world today and his concern that the Muslims are in disarray, unable to cope with the changes taking place in the world, and thus are sliding further and further backwards.

With characteristic directness and aplomb, Dr Mahathir laments the debilitated state of the Muslim world and its apparent inability to help itself to resolve the real problems confronting Muslims. Though endowed with rich resources, he regrets that Muslim countries are unable to put their resources to optimal use to serve and defend Islam and its adherents. He feels that Muslims have done nothing to help themselves. Instead, they have weakened themselves by their constant feuding, their confusing and contradictory interpretations of Islam, and their failure to obey the injunctions of their religion to help themselves.

Dr Mahathir also takes a look at Islam's commitment to justice, Islam as a tolerant and moderate religion, and why Islam is probably the most misunderstood religion often associated with unsavoury activities. He attributes the Muslim condition today in part to ignorance and continuing prejudice against Islam and Muslims. Entering the 21st century, he calls on Muslims to take up the challenges of the Information Age and globalisation. They also need to draw lessons from Islamic history.

This collection of speeches will provide readers with a better understanding of Islam and the Muslim *ummah* Dr Mahathir's sincere, frank, profound and lucid views should make interesting reading.

ISBN 967-978-738-9